EASYRIDERS

Ultimate Custom Bikes

Published in the United States by
THUNDER'S MOUTH PRESS
632 Broadway, Seventh Floor, New York, NY 10012

Cataloging-in-publication data available from the Library of Congress

ISBN 1 56025 151 4

Project Editor: Simon Kirrane
Art Editor: Paul Messam
Design: Danny Defazio
Production: Garry Lewis
Picture Research: Lorna Ainger

Printed and bound in Dubai

10 9 8 7 6 5 4 3 2 1

EASYRIDERS

Ultimate Custom Bikes

K RANDALL BALL

CONTENTS

Chapter One — Street Customs

Chapter Two — Classic & Tourers

Chapter Three — Radical Customs

Chapter Four — Hot Performers

Chapter Five — Choppers Rule

Chapter Six — Gallery

INTRODUCTION

As a young man I dreamed colorful fantasies of flying down endless highways on a custom motorcycle. Gazing at bike magazines was my only outlet into a world separate from my middle-class American life. Until I was 16 I only stumbled onto three fleeting glimpses of truly custom Harley-Davidsons. I wasn't aware of the sheer power I would someday hold in my sunburnt arms, of the sensual sensation of unleashed freedom, the deep feeling of mechanical accomplishment, or the violent world of the outlaw. It was only a wishful dream at the time.

I found that I was completely enthralled by every aspect of the big V-twins, the shape of the bike, the throaty sound, the ticking of a cooling engine, the smell of hot oil. The wild image that motorcycling portrayed sent an anticipatory chill down my anxious youthful spine. I immediately took to sketching motorcycles in my schoolbooks and all over my required homework.

Have you ever experienced 100-plus mph on an open road, blasted between a labyrinth of cars on a congested freeway, or heard the unforgettable sound of handcuffs cinching your wrists together behind your back? If not, there's no way I can explain the exhilaration, the temptation, the challenge, the fear, or the overt frenzy of building and riding a custom motorcycle, but I can offer a colorful fix in the form of this beautifully presented book.

This is a dream book. It affords the reader a carefully selected taste of *Easyriders* magazine, the top magazine in its rowdy market for more than 25 years. *Easyriders* represents the biker lifestyle all over the world. It's distributed in all English-speaking countries, is translated into five languages, and millions of bike enthusiasts read it every month. Its reach and draw offers superlative custom motorcycle talents all across the globe an excellent, dynamic, and controversial vehicle in which to exhibit their

talents to the world. Consequently, the very best chromed, pinstriped, machined, or metal-flaked rolling iron found anywhere shine from the pages of Easyriders, and this is the crème de la crème of those pages, carefully and artistically laid out before your eyes, to savor and enjoy.

This dynamic visual sampling presents two years (1995-1996) of two-wheeled temptation offered as the ultimate one-dimensional tease into a world you may not be aware of. Some 58 of the finest custom motorcycles in the world are lying a few pages away for you to peruse, study, and absorb. We've selected and sorted them into five sparkling sections: Street Custom, Radical Custom, Classic and Touring, Performance Customs, and Choppers. Each chapter gives a brief description of the character and dynamics of each category, then unleashes you on the finest iron imaginable.

For the young novice, hungry for new experiences, this book conjures images found on the edge of reason. Each glossy page comes to life with wild pearlescent paint and long, lean lines reeking of power and mind-altering possibilities. For the experienced builder this is a showcase of custom iron from some of the best builders in the world, packed full of innovations, state-of-the-art products, daring designs, and paint schemes to ponder. For the adult nonrider this is a tease to try something completely different, exciting, youthful, and daring.

All that's lacking in this collection is the actual feel of a rumbling V-twin, the smell of thundering exhaust and burning rubber. We can't imprint these pages with the bellowing crack of a fully built 90-inch, 120-horsepower engine, or the breath-taking lurch as the clutch is released and the wide rear tire rips at the pavement. Unfortunately, we can't simulate the rush of adrenaline you would feel as the front wheel leaves the deck, clawing the air in a wheelstand directed at the neon lights of London's nightlife. We can't paint in words the bone-shaking exhilaration that a racing V-twin imprints on a young person's brain. Nor can we spell out the taste of fear as a siren wails while a rider becomes bathed in flashing red and blue lights because he's been blasting down narrow city streets as if they were the tracks of the autobahn.

You'll find the motorcycle of your dreams contained in these pages, then it's up to you to imagine what you can do to make your dream come true. Ride forever.

—K. Randall Ball

STREET CUSTOMS

Holding the Factory Line

The definition of a street custom is simple, but ever changing, especially in the '90s. In the past, it generally meant the stock Harley frame or chassis had not been modified. In the '80s it signified the same, but a caveat was added. Suddenly, there was a line of aftermarket frames available, frames that, while not stock Harleys, were only moderately modified. The bottom line is that a street custom is a tamer blend of custom Harley.

"To each his own" is the Code of the West when it comes to building custom motorcycles. Many builders associate the street custom with a more ridable modified motorcycle, more street worthy, more reliable, more conservative, etc. I say that's all a crock of bullshit, but that's just my opinion. When the chopper riding biker exploded onto the scene in the '50s the only rule was that there were no rules. That was the code, and any biker worth half his salt would fight anyone who didn't like it.

On the other hand, the original bobbed bikes of the '50s did not sport modified frames, nor were there assortments of aftermarket frames to choose from. Jump to the '90s and many riders would consider a mild custom frame to be a street custom. So, where do we go from here? Well, let's get more specific, or drunk, and forget the whole thing, because beyond all the discussion and details is the long-standing rule: There are no rules, except maybe during the judging segment of some tight-assed bike show. *Easyriders* features them all, from the classic restored scooter to the most radical example of customizing. This book features a wild assortment of all that *Easyriders* represents, but I'm getting away from the primary focus of this section: a discussion of the differences between street customs and the rest of the wild world of choppers.

Bluntly, the traditional street chopper has more creature comforts than radical customs or old-style chops. It may have turn signals, passenger seats, and pegs, large-capacity gas tanks, etc. More than likely it has a standard-length front end. A few inches over or under doesn't make much difference. Many of the standard models available from the Harley-Davidson factory have various front-end lengths. Most street customs have stock raked frames, and are designed reasonably close to a factory configuration. Most have front and rear fenders without major modifications in that area.

Having detailed the major aspects and components of the standard street chopper, keep in mind that this category doesn't generally carry significant performance modifications. However, stroker motors are commonplace in today's growing arena of V-twin performance components. In most cases, if a builder is going to tear down an engine to polish or plate various parts, it's an opportunity to make significant performance modifications during the process. Any modification past performance exhaust, carburetor changes, and ignition alterations to a stroker motor, and the bike will be bumped to the performance section of this book. Blowers, turbochargers, multiple carburetors, fuel ignition, and nitrous bottles would all drive the stroked custom into the performance category.

So there you have it, your complete guide to the conservative, wine tasting, street chopper—motorcycles designed to stay in one piece and carry on the tire-burning relationship long after the first night of tearful hanging on. Or perhaps street customs are designed for the wild man who wants to hang on to that woman he met. The single-seater becomes a bone of contention after about the fourth date. Soon the radical chop that scares the neighbors and frightens small children is relegated to the single guy corner of the garage and another bike is built with class, style, two seats, and warm fuzzy passenger pegs. How the hell would I know? I go through relationships like joggers go through running shoes.

QUIET RIOT

This bike is a confluence of chrome, polished aluminum, and paint. The engine, transmission, primary covers, sheet metal and frame flow into one graceful unit.

This is the first bike in the book, the first street custom, and the first story of sin and chrome. I'm sure worshipping chrome isn't legal in any church, except maybe the temples erected in Harley dealerships to the Harley god. But there is religion on these pages my brothers and sisters, a free worship of all that's modified and shiny, which leads to a no-holds-barred addiction. Say, hallelujah!

It usually begins much as it did for poor, young, and healthy Wes Furrh, who poured his hard-earned paychecks into a brand-new, showroom floor 1992 Fat Boy. All was fine until the next issue of *Easyriders* came out on the newsstands, Wes clamored for a copy, and (dread) read it. Somewhere on those lurid pages were the tempting words,"Say no to stock." As he read on, he discovered the desire to change his reliable, warranty-covered factory motorcycle into something different: a one-off pavement pounder that would make traffic stop, ruin relationships, and make a man's heart race just to look at it.

He studied each feature as if he were searching for the cure to a life-threatening illness. That wasn't enough, though. In the back of the book he noticed an ad for an upcoming motorcycle show. Immediately, he made arrangements to attend, completely ignoring his wife's birthday and marking the end of yet another tenuous biker relationship. As he strolled through the aisles of chrome and perfectly good motorcycles chopped beyond recognition, his level of obsession skyrocketed. With each new concept, component, and modification, his obsession grew stronger.

Rotors and pulleys like these from RC Components have been manufactured out of solid chunks of aluminum to match expensive billet wheel designs.

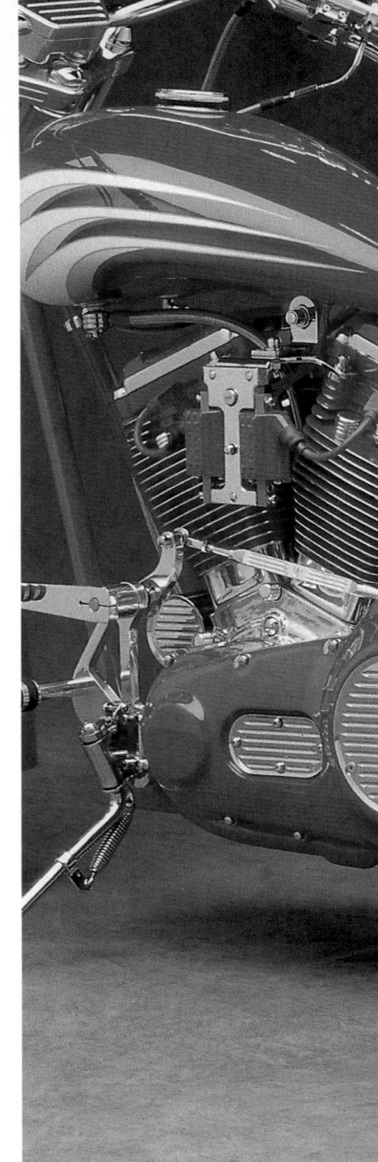

High above him, the Prince of Parts guided this new believer from aftermarket parts manufacturers to engine builders.

Suddenly, he couldn't tolerate the thought of riding a motorcycle with a stock 60-horsepower engine. Without even being introduced to the man, he turned his entire driveline over to Carl Morrow at Carl's Speed Shop, now in Daytona Beach, Florida. Fixated on Arlen Ness designs and components, he made a pilgrimage to the Church of Customizing in pursuit of polished and chromed billet parts.

As if by a guiding light, the Sorcerer of Sleek steered Wes to a builder in Bakersfield, California. A true believer, Bruce LeFevre had only entered the market a couple of years ago, but was building a name fast. One look at the capabilities of Bruce's shop and Wes knew he had found the temple that spoke his language.

Bruce and Wes ripped his new Fat Boy to pieces and began a process (much like Dr. Frankenstein) of taking bits and pieces from graveyards, think-tanks, and chrome baths, and melding them together. Perfectly good, factory-tested fuel cells were stretched and welded. The Department of Transportation-certified safe frame was cut and modified. The Milwaukee-formed fenders were sliced and extended.

Only a man possessed would succumb to such depravity. Wes and Bruce, like two pupils of the Devil, worked incessantly, drowning all their resources into turning a once fine chunk of farm equipment into a work of lust and seduction. What once was timid and acceptable became sensual and sleek. And what once was tame erupted into a speed demon from hell.

Did the two men find the error of their ways? Did they recognize their obsession and repent? Did they find their lost women and apologize, swearing to never polish aluminum again? Hell, no. They're having the time of their lives and now have 10 more bikes to build for new converts. The addiction is growing, as you will witness throughout the pages of this book. God help your soul—ride forever.

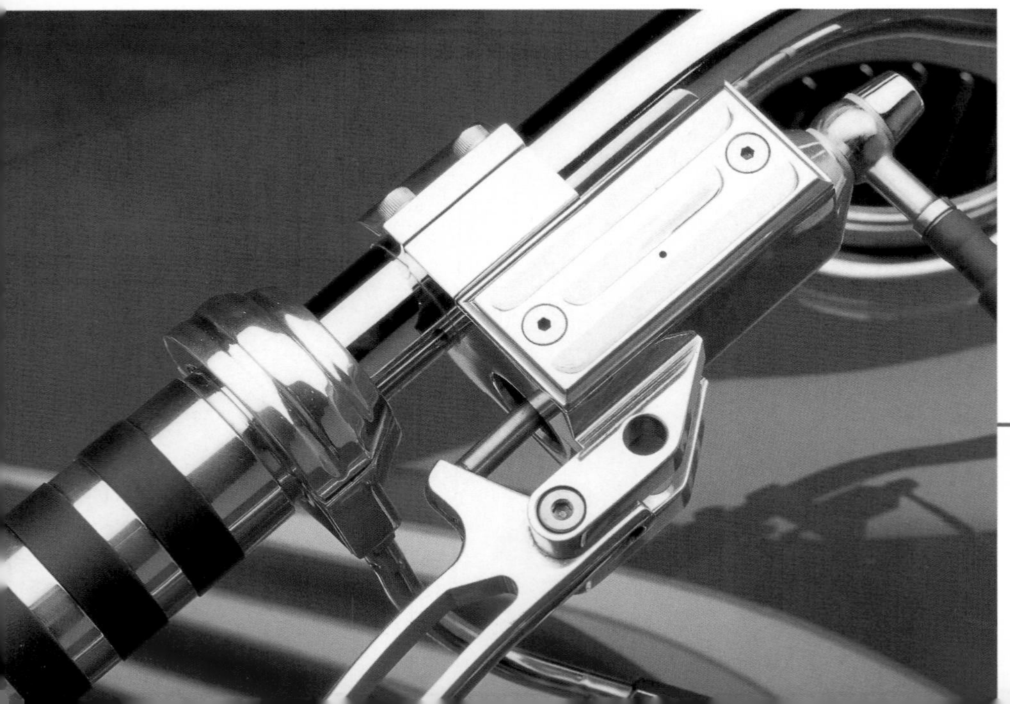

Note the tapered, polished, chromed, or stainless Allen fastener holding the banjo fitting on the Arlen Ness front brake control. Careful attention to detail.

This polished RC Components wheel blends with a polished stainless steel rotor to prevent one expensive component from colliding with another. Then the builder took the time to plug in stainless Allen cap covers into each fastener to top off the detail.

YEAR AND MAKE
1992 Harley-Davidson

OWNER
Wes Furrh

MODEL
Fat Boy

BUILDER
Owner and Bruce LeFevre

ENGINE MODIFICATIONS
Built by Carl's Speed Shop, Dyna S ignition, Wiseco pistons, Carl's heads and cam, S&S Super E carburetor, ThunderHeaders, definned barrels, powdercoated engine components

TRANSMISSION MODIFICATIONS
RC Components wheel sprocket

FINISH
Paint by Bruce LeFevre, red and white Deltron custom mix, special curved scallops by Bruce

FRAME MODIFICATIONS
35-degree rake, 2-inch stretch

FORKS MODIFICATIONS
Painted lower legs, 1¾-inch-over forks

FEATURED
Easyriders, December 1996

The departure from the standard, classical scallop is interesting, but matches perfectly. Note the way the two-dimensional scallops and shadows don't emerge in straight lines, but curve.

LOW, FAT AND FAST

Rigid frames may lack comfy suspension, but there's no chassis that handles with the road like a rigid set low to the ground.

Thirty-year-old Rocky Mountain Roque lives alone in the suburbs of the Mile High City, with his Scotty-built Badster and an everlasting yearning for adventure and women. It's the same drive for many of us in this asphalt world of wine, wild women, and motorcycle thunder.

After a day of wheeling and dealing in the car market, Roque heads to his pad, where this master blaster bike awaits release from solitary confinement in a dark wooden cell. As he pulls into his driveway a transformation begins, a mind-bending alteration that many of us relate to. It's a gradual awakening of evil spirits, like a teenager donning a costume for Halloween, or a gunfighter strapping on dual .45-caliber Colts and heading into the street at sunset.

Roque feels the same surge of adrenaline as he strips off his street clothes and throws on his Levi's, grabs his leather vest and gloves, and heads toward the garage. There's nothing like the night, blasting downtown through pulsating neon on slick streets, with dark adventure concealed around every corner. It all reminds me of my last Shovelhead, although this machine is finer. I got that blood-pumping rush every night as my leathers flapped in the wind and I rolled into the depths of the city. Each night was a new ride in search of hard liquor and loose women.

This motorcycle is a classic street chopper. There's nothing particularly wild about it, but its tight appearance with the short front end and clean black finish give it a timeless ridable flair.

The 103-inch S&S power plant is deceiving in its traditional chassis. It's only the velocity stack on the S&S carburetor, and the shotgun drag pipes give us an indication of the beast within.

LOW, FAT AND FAST

Performance Machine developed complete custom lines of billet aluminum wheels with matching rotors, so a bike owner wouldn't buy an expensive wheel only to cover it with a factory rotor—bad investment.

One particular fall night, I slipped into the city just in time to encounter three drunks coming straight out of a titty bar, slinging rude comments at the girls. The rush of the night and close calls with cages on the urban streets had peaked my senses. I smacked the first bumbling idiot and assisted the bouncer with the removal of the other lewd sots. My quick moves garnered additional respect from the girls—one in particular.

As the short blonde emerged from behind the curtain and one supple leg snaked onto the stage, I knew this was going to be a rewarding experience. Her waist was narrow, cleavage extreme, hair soft as silk and flowing over her shoulders. Her bright blue eyes never left mine, although the room came alive with catcalls and whistles.

"I'm off in an hour," she whispered in my ear, her eyes remaining focused on mine. "I'll be there," I said, my heart beating against my chest. An hour later, we met behind the bar. She was short, but perfectly proportioned, and light as a feather. She straddled my pillion for a wrapped-together ride into the hills. We sipped wine and made love under the stars, and that wasn't the last time I saw her.

That was a handful of years ago, but I can see the same scenario happening to Roque on a weekly basis, and to many bikers like him who know how sensuality moves through the streets at night. Ya gotta love it.

YEAR AND MAKE
1995 Harley-Davidson

OWNER
Roque Armijo

MODEL
Rigid

BUILDER
Scott's Motors, Bob Schenck

ENGINE MODIFICATIONS
Scott-built 103-inch S&S engine, Andrews cam, Super G carburetor, shotgun pipes

TRANSMISSION MODIFICATIONS
Polished case

FINISH
Black, acrylic lacquer, purple scallops with confetti by Vince Unrein

FRAME MODIFICATIONS
Paughco rigid frame, 5-degree rake, 2-inch stretch

FRONT END MODIFICATIONS
Marzocchi forks, Pro Street mid glide, billet aluminum triple trees

FEATURED
Easyriders, February 1996

LOW BOY

From a distance this bike has seemingly stock lines, but as you close in, the execution of finely finished detail jumps until you can't get enough of the deep paint and even deeper metal finish.

This motorcycle is one of the finest examples of street customs I've ever come across, predominantly due to the extremely high level of detail and finish. Damon's bike studio, with George Sepulveda urging them on, took what was going to be a simple repaint order then stripped the stock Softail to the bone. Seems George raced dirt bikes in his younger days, then Harleys caught his eye. He pondered and scratched his tail until a neighbor put his hardly used Softail on the market. George made a deal and took over the factory original. He rode the beast daily, experiencing the new world of the free thinking Harley rider.

Unfortunately, his bike was not experiencing the same transformation. His buddies still referred to the machine as his neighbor's bike, finally telling George, "You'll need to piss on it before it's yours, man."

George scratched some more and pondered the implications of pissing on the bike. Surely, it would rust the chrome, he thought. Then on a ride through town he pulled into the well-known think tank/custom studio of Damon's. The custom wizards pointed out that pissing on his bike wasn't a literal definition, but a euphemism for altering it to suit personal tastes. "Leave the pissing for the dogs and fire hydrants," Tom, the proprietor, told George.

George decided on a paint scheme and turned the bike over to the capable hands of Tom and his crew. But the two of them never stopped at the paint. As sheet metal finishing reached completion, George studied the subtle techniques embodied in the paint and was so taken back by the artistic value, the overwhelming talent, and stunning finish, that as it stood, he could no longer bolt the sheet metal to his motorcycle.

To maintain a pristine appearance, pipe shields have been carefully designed to cover any unsightly bluing. A full array of Ness accessories insures that the engine looks top-notch.

The caliber of the paint job demanded a fighting conversion. From that point on the machine became a family odyssey. George's wife, India, and their oldest son, Daniel, became overnight Harley aficionados. The frame was raked slightly, the fenders modified, and the tanks stretched to enhance the paint scheme. The frame needed a touch up, even though it was repainted stock black. The attention to detail in removing blemishes and smoothing the shape of the rails translated into the perfect black frame. George and his son studied accessories and began to outfit the bike with matching polished billet wheels, rotors and pulleys. Every spacer and fastener was chromed. All the lines were replaced with braided steel. The engine was disassembled, completely polished, and outfitted with Arlen Ness accessories and fresh chrome. From a distance the bike appears factory, but the closer the eye gets, the more custom finesse is seen to adorn this rolling red rocket.

The Softail made its debut at the *Easyriders* Bike Show in Anaheim, California, where it took Best of Show in the Street Custom Class. From the leather-braided grips to match the final finish, to the small stainless steel caps that detail all the Allen bolt fasteners, this bike is about as sanitary as the mess on the admiral's flagship (and, believe me, that ain't very sanitary).

LOW BOY

Here's another classic case of detail-mania. A man goes into a shop to get a paint job and wham! Look at that engine. Every element is polished and chromed.

Even the belt guard was carefully selected to conform with the Sun Devil billet aluminum wheel and matching pulley and rotor; then everything was polished to a mirror finish.

YEAR AND MAKE
1991 Harley-Davidson

OWNER
George Sepulveda

MODEL
Low Boy Softail

ENGINE MODIFICATIONS
89-cubic-inch S&S motor, S&S 561 cam, S&S carburetor, ThunderHeader exhaust, Crane HI-4 ignition

TRANSMISSION MODIFICATIONS
Backcut gears

FINISH
Multi-colored candy apple red, ghost graphics, paint by Damon's, Southern California

FRAME MODIFICATIONS
1991 Harley-Davidson, raked 7 degrees

FRONT END MODIFICATIONS
Wide glide, all chromed, Custom Chrome turn signals, Headwinds headlight, chromed controls

FEATURED
Easyriders, November 1996

EXCELLENCE & ENDURANCE

Raked slightly, the trimmed front end still handles in a sporty fashion. The painted gauge housings tie the paint scheme to the front end.

Here's another example of dedication to the lifestyle. This bike was the first model of the new line of Harley-Davidson Dyna Glides. Chip "Big Daddy" Latimer from Chicago stood in his local dealership, stared at the Sportster-looking, rubbermounted chassis, and wondered what Chris Burchinal of Anaheim, California, could do to customize it.

Chris builds one-of-a-kind motorcycles with a go-fast flare. So Big Daddy sent Burchinal a new-model challenge. The Dyna Glide landed on Chris' doorstop still in the crate. His instructions: "Make it cool and make it move." Chris dove into the project like a man with a new woman

Dyna Glides represent the latest in rubbermount technology. The factory returned to the early swingarm design and rolled away from the FXR frame configuration. In the process, the frame became bulky and the seat height was too high, eliminating the line most builders reach for.

"By the time the bike was finished, I had built and rejected several tanks and rear fenders, to say nothing of the hours spent reworking the frame, doing detail work on the swingarm and so forth," Chris said.

Chris fights to keep his dream alive, but the man loves what he does for a living. That's the key, you know, loving what you're doing.

Chris did an excellent job of detailing by shaping the taillight into a flared fender, then adding narrowed turn signals to the fender rails and painting the system to match so as not to interrupt frame's line.

EXCELLENCE & ENDURANCE

Dyna Glides are tough to customize due to the top of the frame being very flat. Several builders have attempted various modifications, unsuccessfully, but Chris Burchinal succeeded in giving this high-tech Dyna a Sporty look.

YEAR AND MAKE
1991 Harley-Davidson

OWNER
Chip Latimer

MODEL
Sturgis Dyna Glide

BUILDER
Burchinal's, Anaheim, California

ENGINE MODIFICATIONS
89 cubic inches, S&S 4 5/8 stroke, Dyna single-fire ignition, Feuling heads, Leineweber cam, Dell 'Orto carb, Mike Hamm exhaust, SuperTrapp muffler

TRANSMISSION MODIFICATIONS
Andrews back-cut gears and trans sprocket

FINISH
Molding by Mahood's Body and Paint, Xcalibur paint, poly enamel material

FRAME MODIFICATIONS
Burchinal's modified Dyna Glide, swingarm by Burchinal's, 33-degree rake

FRONT END MODIFICATIONS
39mm narrow Harley-Davidson glide, shortened, triple trees by Burchinal's

FEATURED
Easyriders, June 1995

TIZ BAD

This is Dave Kennedy's first bike, although he sold it several years ago as he was rolling his love for Harleys into a full-time career. Later, he had the fortune to retrieve his first love, though she was in somewhat rough condition.

He felt the fever and it set his life's course in the business of building bikes, but when he bought the '78 Shovelhead back, he lost his mind. The rule of thumb in building bikes is to create flow and continuity. That works for most, but sporadically a man slips a cog and goes too far. Dave did.

For instance, you're not supposed to mix custom elements: Don't use more than two finishes on the engine. Chrome and powdercoat, okay. Polish and black-wrinkle works nice. But no one, I mean no one, black wrinkles the cylinders, powdercoats the heads a different color, adds gold highlights to the chrome, then throws in a handful of black anodized and engraved accessories. Engraving belongs on dinnerware, guns, and girls.

To top it off, the various blue hues on the heads, brake calipers and rotors don't match the finish on the frame and sheetmetal. Then there's more gold. Take off all the gold and engraving, chrome the parts and return them to the machine, and it would spring to life as a real motorcycle–a motorcycle meant to beat pavement, beat cars, and beat the other guys to the strip joints.

A whirlwind of finishes, this bike is a display counter overflowing with chromed, polished, anodized, engraved, and gold-plated components.

Despite Dave's unorthodox approach he has created a machine that sits well with other great custom bikes.

YEAR AND MAKE
1978 Harley-Davidson

OWNER
Dave Kennedy

MODEL
FXWG

BUILDER
Dave Kennedy

ENGINE MODIFICATIONS
90-cubic-inch Shovelhead, S&S 4 3/4 stroke, Dyna single-fire ignition, Rivera heads, Rivera SU carburetor, Python Pipes

TRANSMISSION MODIFICATIONS
Andrews close-ratio gears

FINISH
Royal blue metalflake, owner molded and painted, illustration and striping

FRAME MODIFICATIONS
Stock Harley-Davidson, molding and paint by owner

FRONT END MODIFICATIONS
Harley-Davidson FXWG glide front end, shortened 2 inches, Arlen Ness triple trees, gold details

FEATURED
Easyriders, January 1996

THE TIGER

A trimmed Pro Street chassis is the basis for this custom with handformed touches such as the rear and front fenders, the stretched gas tank, and contoured oil tank.

This bike represents one of the most popular custom configurations on the market today. Two members of our staff ride Pro Street bikes. The genius behind the design is Californian Kenny Boyce. He creates the chassis and builds bikes around them. The key is the frame. Builders have created fat Pro Streets, racing Pro Streets, big-fendered Pro Streets, you name it, they've made it. The design of each and every machine begins with the frame.

This incredible example was constructed at the *Easyriders* store in Columbus, Ohio, to be a mascot bike. Doug Jahnke, a master fabricator and 16-year veteran behind spray guns took on the challenge, designing the shop bike around Kenny's frame. As you can see, Doug eliminated all forward controls for a clean appearance and a more jockey-style riding position. He reworked a Softail oil tank to conform with the lines of the Pro Street frame and manufactured a gas tank to fit the design to a tee. It's made from steel as are the Doug-built fenders.

There's only one element of this particular bike I don't understand—the paint. Who the hell said they should paint a bike shop pink! All right, someone out there has had the pumped-up vocabulary to call the damn thing fuschia, but I don't care if they call it misty rose, or even a virgin's kiss—it's still pink!

THE TIGER

Simple Performance Machine wheels and brakes add the light billet look to the shaved front end, which features Ness billet components and chrome—super clean.

YEAR AND MAKE
1995 Harley-Davidson

OWNER
Doug Jahnke

MODEL
Pro Street

BUILDER
Doug Jahnke

ENGINE MODIFICATIONS
80 cubic inches, rebuilt by T.R. Reiser of Easyriders of Columbus, Dyna S ignition, Power House cases, Crane cam, S&S Super E carburetor, Jammer dual drag pipes.

TRANSMISSION MODIFICATIONS
JayBrake shifting, 32-tooth trans sprocket, 70-tooth rear wheel pulley

FINISH
Molding by Doug Jahnke, painting by Doug, Deltron fuschia paint, tiger stripe graphics

FRAME MODIFICATIONS
1994 Kenny Boyce frame, 30.5-degree rake, trimmed by Doug

FRONT END MODIFICATIONS
Narrow glide, shortened 4 inches, chromed, custom billet triple trees, Headwinds headlight

FEATURED
Easyriders, December 1995

HEARTS ON FIRE

I've met many bike builders in my time. Some of the best are multi-talented, while others have specialties or individual skills.

A few builders are experts in what I call "finished detailing." And the master of supreme detailing throughout the industry is Don Hotop from Madison, Iowa. When you receive one of his bikes, you won't want to touch it for years.

Well, this bike belongs to a builder who has been taking serious note of Don's abilities and his attention to detail. Few builders purchase expensive custom brake calipers, dismantle them, have the faces shaved, then machine in their own distinctive design to flow with the rest of the bike's components. John Bryant did just that with this machine. He took extra care to have the tanks completely conceal frame members. There are no ugly gaps, no unsightly tabs to worry about, and all the components match. There's no mistaking, this is a finely detailed machine, and it makes a difference.

With quality detail work comes careful, well thought out assembly. Check the design machined into the derby and cone covers. Now check the tail light, the brake calipers, the chain guard, and the starter motor. Not only did John go to the time and expense to create and engineer each component for his brother-in-law, Fred Angie's, motorcycle project, but he had each element painted to match the overall paint scheme. The result is a burning flame on two wheels... a tribute to detail.

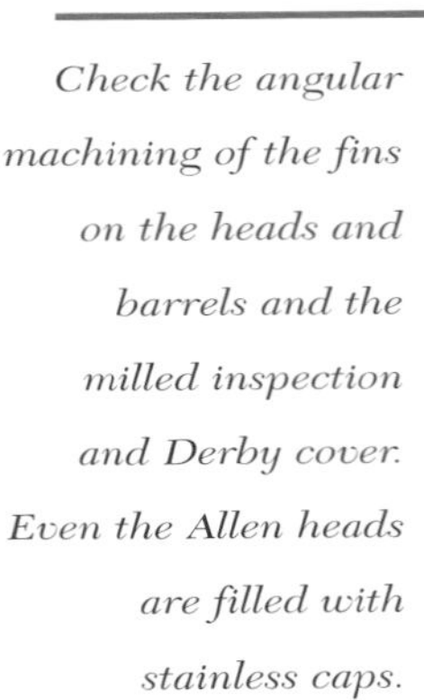

Check the angular machining of the fins on the heads and barrels and the milled inspection and Derby cover. Even the Allen heads are filled with stainless caps.

This bike is tight in the detail department. Care and attention are evident in the fit of the tanks, fenders, air dam, and the intricate machining.

YEAR AND MAKE
1975 Harley-Davidson

OWNER
Fred Angie

MODEL
FXE

BUILDER
John Bryant Motorcycle Engineering

ENGINE MODIFICATIONS
90-cubic-inch stroker, S&S wheels, Carillo rods, S&S pistons, ported and polished heads, Headquarters .530 lift cam, Dell 'Orto carburetor, John Bryant pipes, Velva-Touch lifters, Strader Engineering mufflers

TRANSMISSION MODIFICATIONS
Polished cases

FINISH
Molding by Lane Davis, Viper Red Sikkens urethane paint by JSI Collision Centers, special paint by Doug Jahnke

FRAME MODIFICATIONS
Bryant/Davis modified Harley-Davidson frame, 33-degree rake, 2-inch stretch

FRONT END MODIFICATIONS
Shortened 2 inches, handmade triple trees and caps by Bryant

FEATURED
Easyriders, May 1996

THE RIGHT TRACK

Here's the epitome of a street custom: a stock Harley-Davidson accessorized tastefully while maintaining the original configuration. This is Tod Couch's first Harley, and like many other builders on tight budgets, he bought himself a basket case with a dream of building a running Harley.

His notion at the time didn't involve street custom design; he just wanted to get the bike running. Tod began by cleaning and polishing parts. He bought a 1½-horsepower polishing motor, picked up half of the engine case, and went to work. There's a certain elixir quality to building and detailing bikes. A mad scientist mentality takes over as you lean that soft aluminum case against a spinning polishing wheel. With each new glimmering surface, Tod was moved—no, driven—to polish more and more.

Dull pieces took on a life of their own as he became hell-bent to fill the garage he shared with his roommates with polishing fibers. His bros complained of the high-speed motor screaming into the wee hours of the night, but Tod was relentless, entering the house at all hours covered in a fine soot, a chromed glint in his eyes and a smirk on his face after completing another transformation.

When the paint finally returned from Horst, Tod was duly impressed and decided that a couple of elements on the engine should match the paint scheme. The end result is an undiluted, pure street chopper.

A single man's first project, Tod added simple polished detail and a handful of tasteful accessories to create a compact, ridable custom

This builder, so impressed with his Horst paint job, added bits of the same color to his spark plug wires, derby cover, and engine detail.

YEAR AND MAKE
1978 Harley-Davidson

OWNER
Tod Couch

MODEL
FXE

BUILDER
Owner

ENGINE MODIFICATIONS
Cases blended and polished, heads ported and polished, Andrews C cam, Weber 40 DCOE carburetor, Cycle Shack pipes, K&N air cleaner

TRANSMISSION MODIFICATIONS
None

FINISH
Molding by Tod, paint by Horst, blue urethane with Horst Graphics

FRAME MODIFICATIONS
Molded and powdercoated

FRONT END MODIFICATIONS
2-inches under, billet caps, chrome

FEATURED
Easyriders, December 1995

ARIZONA SUNSET

Rain is infrequent in Scottsdale, Arizona. The sun shines most of the time, and many of the residents would rather it take an occasional vacation as the temperature crests the 120-degree mark. Now watch me make a clever link with that bit of trivia into something meaningful.

The blazing sun of the Arizona desert was the inspiration for the dazzling paint scheme of this Pro Street custom. Myron Larrabee, a riding partner of mine, is the owner, with his wife, Cindy (who keeps things going so Myron can play, work out, and build bikes), owns *Easyriders* of Scottsdale and a couple of World Gyms in the area. Myron was once Mr. Arizona, the body building champion.

This man understands and lives with discipline.

We rode with Myron to Sturgis last year. He didn't have anything particular to ride so he bought a fresh Road King, chromed and detailed absolutely everything, rebuilt the engine, stroked it, and off we went. Helluva ride. But he wouldn't have gone unless he had a completely detailed bike to take. He's that kind of guy, persnickety, with a propensity for perfection.

This Pro Street bike is indicative of that constant desire and dedication to detail. In fact, I'm always a bit nervous to show him anything of mine, for fear it won't measure up. On the other hand, after a few hundred miles of bugs, dirt, and dust, who can see the details?

Let's ride!

This Pro Street custom embodies handling, high speed, and today's high-tech components. Not only is it a kick to ride, but it draws a crowd.

ARIZONA SUNSET

Note the Dawn Holmes painted face on the speedometer, the tapering Arizona sunset to the paint treatment, and the billet accessories.

YEAR AND MAKE
1995 Harley-Davidson

OWNER
Myron Larrabee

MODEL
Pro Street

BUILDER
Easyriders of Scottsdale

ENGINE MODIFICATIONS
90-cubic-inch stroker, S&S wheels, 96-cubic-inch stroker, Delkron cases, S&S wheels and rods, RevTech heads, S&S carb and cam, Dyna single-fire ignition and Bub exhaust

TRANSMISSION MODIFICATIONS
Andrews gears, rebuilt by Zippers, Performance Machine shifting

FINISH
Molding by Denny Bloom, paint by Denny Bloom, yellow to purple PPG paint

FRAME MODIFICATIONS
Kenny Boyce Pro Street frame, fat tire model, 5-degree rake, 2 1/2-inch stretch

FRONT END MODIFICATIONS
Arlen Ness triple trees, dual disc brake mounts, rebuilt and chromed by *Easyriders* of Scottsdale

FEATURED
Easyriders, November 1995

TITMOBILE

Visalia, California, is as hot as a spray of pepper in the face during summer, and is home to the edge of the northern California wine country. I rode through this tinderbox a half-dozen times each summer, holding my breath for the time when I could see the coast and feel the fresh salt breeze off the Pacific.

I never knew that the town on Highway 99, which I blasted through as if my ass were on fire, contained the men who invented the Double D headlight featured on this bike. And I didn't know that the owner of this bike partnered with his dad to make this headlight dream come true. I also didn't know that while I lay in the Paso Robles Hospital some 85 miles away, because I was so drunk on Southern Comfort I couldn't turn my stretched cop bike around in the street, that Tim's inspiration was his other partner's '37 Packard headlight.

Hell, I didn't even know that his partner, Butch Reed, made this masterpiece come to life. I was never told that this creative partnership between a friend and a father wouldn't have happened if it weren't for the owner of Jimmy Z's Upholstery Shop in Visalia, who introduced the two. How was I to know? I was passed out in the Hospital while a bunch of unsympathetic nurses cut off my favorite Levi's just to save my ass—the audacity of their behavior.

The 1965 Panhead was built specifically to showcase the double-D headlight that Tim Thiel developed along with a couple of friends and his father.

Classic lines, tight detailing, careful accessory selection, and a very complementary paint scheme make this a standout machine wherever it goes.

YEAR AND MAKE
1965 Harley-Davidson

OWNER
Timothy Thiel

MODEL
Electra Glide

BUILDER
TR Customs

ENGINE MODIFICATIONS
84-inch S&S stroker, Andrews B-Grind cam, SU carburetor, Paughco exhaust, Custom Chrome mufflers

TRANSMISSION MODIFICATIONS
Rebuilt by Kurt and Tim

FINISH
Dale Kelley molding and paint, Thompson/PBE Lincoln white and BMW purple

FRAME MODIFICATIONS
Early swingarm

FRONT END MODIFICATIONS
Original wide glide, 2-inch-under tubes, big boob headlight shroud by TR Customs

FEATURED
Easyriders, September 1996

This bike is an interesting confluence of eras. At first it appears to be almost factory original but then the custom seat, gold highlights, exotic manifold, and flames give way to the custom world.

FLASHY FAT BOY

Ron Simms of Bay Area Custom Cycles builds all of his bikes low and wide with Performance Machine brakes and wheels—all polished or chromed billet aluminum.

You want tough, nasty, terrifying motorcycles? Then you need to talk to Ron Simms, the owner of Bay Area Custom Cycles in Hayward, California. His reputation is as a tough guy who's been building bikes for more than 20 years. If you don't like his style, hit the road. Some guys are afraid to walk alone through the door of his shop.

His custom recipe generally includes wide rear tires on Paughco Softail frames, with Performance Machine billet wheels and brakes, heavily stroked motors almost exclusively built with S&S components, an assortment of Ron's own collection of billet aluminum parts, and a low-slung Corbin seat. I've seen any number of other builders attempt to duplicate his style, but it never comes across correctly. His machines are bad, mean, and tough, and Ron's pavement splitters tear up the miles from coast to coast. You never see the man at an event without 25 fresh creations surrounding him.

Joey Scott, a television producer, is the perfect example of a man looking for a builder who walks his walk. He bought his first H-D five years ago and began to customize it. "I bolted on an entire aftermarket catalog," Joey said, "and I still wasn't happy." He looked around for someone who could speak to his style and stumbled on Ron's display at a show. One look at the nasty, bas-ass bikes was all it took.

The contemporary Horst paint job is coupled with a series of slotted gadgets that string together the cohesive style of the motorcycle.

YEAR AND MAKE
1994 Harley-Davidson

OWNER
Joey Scott

MODEL
Electra Glide

BUILDER
Ron Simms, Bay Area Custom Cycles (BACC)

ENGINE MODIFICATIONS
98-inch stroker built by Bob Gomes, S&S lower end, STD cases, Sifton cam, Thunder Header exhaust

TRANSMISSION MODIFICATIONS
Polished cases, BACC accessories

FINISH
Molding and painting by Horst, purple exploding teal, special paint by Horst

FRAME MODIFICATIONS
Paughco Softail frame modified by BACC, widened, 37-degree rake, BACC swingarm

FRONT END MODIFICATIONS
Harley-Davidson wide glide, 2-inch-over tubes, modified by Steve Nichols, BACC trees

FEATURED
Easyriders, February, 1995

Many of the accessories, such as the massive billet swingarm and the matching fender rails, come directly from the Bay Area Custom Cycles think-tank.

NERVE MEDICINE

This bike is as tough as it looks. Built low with ground-hugging fenders, it's powered with 103 inches of stroked force plumbed to a fingertip nitrous system.

The rear of this machine has the demeanor of a lowered Cadillac. The rear fender was widened to complement the Ness front fender.

This machine offers a unique combination of styles. It's slammed down like a Chevy low rider. It's a fast, pro-street drag bike. It's as wide as a Ron Simms' custom, and as tough. It's a tight, lean mixture of everything mean on the market.

Owner Mark Cohen made an interesting comment during the photo shoot. He pointed out that this bike and his other customs are all collaborative efforts. Thinking about this, I realized that there are few of the "one-man show" bike builders left around. Twenty-five years ago, I built my bikes from scratch pretty much by myself. I rebuilt the engines, fabricated the parts, assembled the bikes, and tuned and maintained them. A machine shop bored my cylinders and ground the valves. I needed a chromer, but I avoided them, and I needed parts. I did the rest myself. But times change and custom creators discovered, as Mark did, that the experts of engine performance and wizards of custom paint are ready, willing, and able to make your two-wheeled fantasies come true in ways that only improve your original concept.

So Mark's dead-on correct in saying that each custom is a collaborative effort with many talents lending a hand to create award-winning customs. Although rumor has it that Mark has been seen in his garage at 4 a.m. pouring over a new creation. "It's the perfect tonic for relieving stress," said Mark.

Even the polished and plated engine components look tough. The slotted accessories and transmission covers give the motor the machined look. The nasty velocity stack allows all the power to show.

YEAR AND MAKE
1994 Harley-Davidson

OWNER
Mark Cohen

BUILDER
Owner

ENGINE MODIFICATIONS
103-inch S&S stroker, Delkron cases, Dyna S ignition, Branch IV heads, S&S Super G carburetor, Wink's Customs exhaust, NOS

TRANSMISSION MODIFICATIONS
Sputhe door, polished case, Andrews gears, RC Components wheel sprocket

FINISH
Painting and molding by Joe at FLC, teal, purple, magenta by House of Kolor

FRAME MODIFICATIONS
Tripoli Softail chassis, 35-degree rake, 1-inch stretch, widened and offset

FRONT END MODIFICATIONS
W.P. Roma inverted forks, milled and polished

FEATURED
Easyriders, May 1996

DRIVE BYE

Ah, a true street custom. Why? Let's take a look. The classic frame is completely box stock with the exception of the paint job. Unlike many of the other customs shining forth from this book, this bike is not only a collaboration of efforts and talents, but an accumulation of different parts from various years.

The top of the engine is from one year, the bottom part is from another, and the transmission is from still another place in time all together.

For years, decades even, Harley parts were interchangeable. In fact, it wasn't until the late '80s that the factory discovered built-in obsolescence. Strictly speaking, the term stands for purposefully making parts that wear out in a designated amount of time. I don't believe the factory operates under this dictum, but they have made it more difficult to exchange parts from year to year, forcing customers to head back to the dealership more often.

But, let's get back to Kerry's classic masterpiece, featuring bullet holes painted by the daVinci of custom paint creations, Horst. In order to duplicate the real thing on Kerry's sheet metal, Horst actually took a painted fender into his yard and blasted away Nice work, huh?

It's a classic street custom that truly stands out in the crowd.

DRIVE BYE

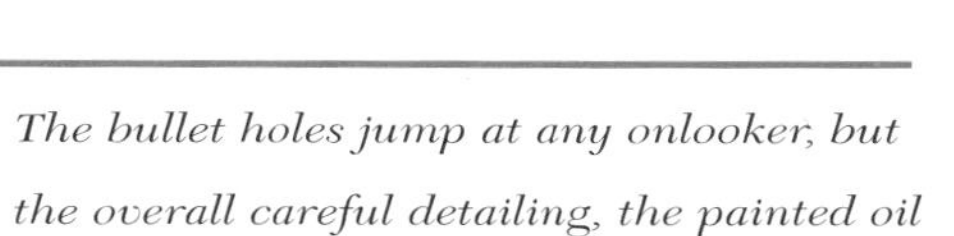

The bullet holes jump at any onlooker, but the overall careful detailing, the painted oil tank, the chromed components, and the slim seat pull the machine together.

This builder used predominately stock Harley-Davidson parts to accomplish this design, with the exception of the molded dash, the exhaust system, and the baby ape handlebars.

YEAR AND MAKE
1993 Pan/Shovel

OWNER
Kerry Puccio

MODEL
80-inch FL

BUILDERS
Puccio and Villegas

ENGINE MODIFICATIONS
Richard Williams 80-inch Shovel lower end, ported and polished heads, Crane cam, S&S carburetor, Puccio Welding exhaust, Arias pistons

TRANSMISSION MODIFICATIONS
1972 Harley-Davidson 4-speed gear box, belt drive

FINISH
Molding by Renteria Bros, paint by Horst and Renteria Bros, blood red paint by Deltron, bullet holes by Horst

FRAME MODIFICATIONS
None

FRONT END MODIFICATIONS
Polished wide glide, lowered 1 inch

FEATURED
Easyriders, July 1995

LOW PROFILER

Here's a true budget custom. It was built by a friend of mine who won't be offended if I reveal what a cheap bastard he is. But now that I think of it, the last time E.Z. was offended he wasn't so "easy." As it comes back to me, I realize that he was downright harsh on the dude who offended him; if fact, I cringe to think about that night, the blood, the ambulance...

Perhaps I should stick to a story line packed with detailed accolades, outlining E.Z.'s long and colorful history in the custom bike business. But what the hell, he's older now, maybe he's mellowed. Let's live on the edge, just like we do every time we put one of these monsters in gear and head out on the highway.

This scoot is an excellent example of how anyone can build a totally unique scooter without severe cash outlays. Take a close look at E.Z.'s $100 flat black paint job, the unfinished bare engine (no chrome, no billet aluminum accessories, no polish, no powdercoating, and no electronic ignition—just points). Look over the wheels. They are bargain basement stock aluminum wheels (no chrome, no polish, no powdercoating, and no black wrinkle). Hey, he was even too cheap to pay for a license plate bracket, so he glued it to the back of his seat.

But ya gotta admit that the bike does have style.

The engine is factory stock and bare bones—nothing polished, chromed, or black wrinkled. Just bolt her in and go. Well, almost.

LOW PROFILER

After all the chrome and glitter here's a custom machine that looks homegrown with its flat black, flat aluminum, and flat chrome appearance.

A trouble-free build, this machine avoided thousand of hours for paint, polish, and chrome preparation.

YEAR AND MAKE
1993 E.Z. Special

OWNER
E.Z. Winarsky

MODEL
Custom Toy

BUILDER
Owner

ENGINE MODIFICATIONS
Sifton 143 cam, QwikSilver carburetor, modified Linkert air cleaner, Ness and SuperTrapp exhaust

TRANSMISSION MODIFICATIONS
Close ratio gears, jockey shift

FINISH
Molding by owner, painted by owner and Jack, semi-flat black paint and billet wheel trim

FRAME MODIFICATIONS
Santee/Custom Chrome swingarm frame, 3-degree rake, 2 1/4-inch stretch, welds frenched

FRONT END MODIFICATIONS
Standard wide glide, 2 inches over, Custom Chrome trees

FEATURED
Easyriders, May 1996

OUT OF THE BLUE

*Easyriders has kicked off a franchise store operation. These stores, which sport the *Easyriders* name, offer everything that factory dealerships distance themselves from. Factory spells stock, left alone motorcycles to be ridden like post office employees drive those little trucks. It's no wonder that postal employees go mad on occasion and try to rid the earth of their fellow brain-dead co-workers.

Easyriders stores are the opposite of conservative dealerships. They're founded on the rock-solid principles of personal freedom, artistic creativity, lane-splitting performance, and nonstop imagination. *Easyriders* stores allow the average bland biker the opportunity to add a little color to his life, to fill his nights with high-speed thrills, and to find a divorce attorney quick.

This blue beast was created by a group of builders and visionaries at the *Easyriders* store in Fresno California. It's difficult to imagine that this wild ride began as a boring factory tractor. Just the paint job, modified fenders with LED taillights, and hand-fabricated headlight housing bring this blue sky scoot to life. After adding the heavily molded frame, billet wheels with Performance Machine brakes, braided lines, and heavily detailed driveline, this machine was transformed from a two-wheeled tractor to an adrenaline-pumping sex machine.

Easyriders *of Fresno, California, built this machine as a showcase custom. It accurately displays their talents, style, and desire to impress the opposite sex.*

Note the paint work designed to give the impression of deep metal fabrication. No stretch to the tanks, but the custom dash brings the fuel cells together.

LED taillights afford riders superior lighting and customizers flexible customizing alternatives. In this case, a mixture of Performance Machine brakes and Boyd's wheels make the chassis roll and stop.

YEAR AND MAKE
1989 Harley-Davidson

OWNER
Phil Parnagian

MODEL
Heritage Softail

BUILDER
Easyriders of Fresno, Dennis Parnagian/Neil Averril, Prescision Cycle

ENGINE MODIFICATIONS
89-cubic-inch stroker, Crane ignition, Wiseco pistons, Crane cam, S&S Super E carburetor, Arlen Ness pipes, Sumax air cleaner

TRANSMISSION MODIFICATIONS
None

FINISH
Molding by Neil Averril, paint by Neil and Jim Ogawa, blue, pearl urethane

FRAME MODIFICATIONS
1989 Harley-Davidson Softail frame, raked to 38 degrees, extensive molding, modified Rick Doss air cleaner

FRONT END MODIFICATIONS
Harley-Davidson Wide Glide, Johnny Pagnini triple trees, all chrome

FEATURED
VQ magazine, February 1997

STURGIS GOLD

Note the front end and the slot cut in the rear legs. In an age of unlimited custom parts a builder must modify the aftermarket accessory to suit his or her tastes for a truly original look.

I'm sure there are people out there who believe a man plans out his bike, orders the parts, sends them out for paint, and when they return, pops that sucker together and goes for a ride. That's hardly ever the case.

In this case, Ultra Custom Cycles made this dream machine and Sturgis Custom Bike Show winner come alive for Andy and Joyce Aponte. "It came apart and went together so many times for fitting and refitting that Frank could build it with his eyes closed," said Kraig from Ultra Custom Cycles.

In addition to everyday components, they created customized doodads such as the handmade feathers on the front of the winged wheel. Besides unique styling, the wing effect promotes cooling to the engine and was built to allow the owner to remove them easily for maintenance or repainting. And as you might imagine, such fabrication takes considerable time.

Everything must fit, and if you're of the mind to hide away components from their standard positions, a lot of thought needs to go into each application. Note the stretched tanks and the panels at the rear of the frame. I'm sure they bolted this puppy together and put a few miles on it before the chromer and painter got their hands on it.

Spoked wheels have gone custom by adding more spokes. Pat Kennedys Custom Cycles creates 80- and 120-spoke wheels with custom stainless hubs and spokes, twisted spokes, and chrome, stainless, aluminum, and nipple-less rims.

YEAR AND MAKE
1994 Special Construction

OWNER
Andy and Joyce Aponte

MODEL
Hardtail Indian

BUILDER
Ultra Custom Cycles

ENGINE MODIFICATIONS
96-cubic-inch S&S engine, dual Karata mags, rebuilt by Frank Marrero, S&S 563 cam, Dell 'Orto carburetor, drag pipes

TRANSMISSION MODIFICATIONS
Close ratio gears

FINISH
Molding by Al Hellerud, painting by Steve Beam, black acrylic urethane paint, murals by Carlos

FRAME MODIFICATIONS
36-degree rake, 2-inch stretch

FRONT END MODIFICATIONS
4-inch-under-stock springer

FEATURED
Easyriders, April 1996

WHERE THERE'S SMOKE

This is a standard Harley-Davidson Softail, repainted and adorned with accessories to assist with the marketing of Camel Cigarettes. This is a commonplace marketing scheme for many companies. Nothing captures onlookers' attention like a custom Harley.

With the popularity of this American icon on the rise, many companies have chosen Harleys to represent them in one way or another. Not only are they eye-catching, they're also easy to move around and store as "promotional vehicles." RJ Reynolds agreed with this concept, but, like any major corporation, it took them down to the last minute to obtain a consensus from their board as to the direction of their Camel Cigarette bike.

Once the vote was counted and the direction determined, the motion

Little touches like the tank emblem, embroidered seat, stained-glass taillight, and special paint make this bike come alive.

began. An executive called up a laid-off ad exec. who rides and asked for guidance. Since the kid was out of a job and hanging out at Bob "Magoo" Mendel's Motorcycle Frame Up Ltd. (long name), he recommended that the frightened executive have a career discussion with Bob. They had 22 days to complete the bike, which didn't exist, in order to display it in Daytona Beach before a half-million smokin' bikers.

A couple of days later, a brand-new Fat Boy was delivered to the shop in a crate. Everything in the shop stopped, with the exception of this project, which went into late-night, weekend, and even lunch-break overtime.

The Camel-themed Harley with the stained glass tail-light was a complete success on the shores of Daytona, and then went on to grab attention at Myrtle Beach, South Carolina, Laconia, New Hampshire, and Asheville, North Carolina.

Wherever it appears, bikers agree that this scoot is "smokin"!

YEAR AND MAKE
1993 Harley-Davidson

OWNER
RJ Reynolds

MODEL
Fat Boy

BUILDER
Bob "Magoo" Mendel

ENGINE MODIFICATIONS
Dyna S single-fire ignition, Wiseco 10.5:1 pistons, cases and heads polished, Andrews 468 cam, S&S E carburetor, Samson exhaust, Arlen Ness lifter blocks

TRANSMISSION MODIFICATIONS
Ness accessories

FINISH
Paint by Swanny, desert beige, mocha brown, harvest gold urethane, handpainted mural by Swanny

FRAME MODIFICATIONS
Powdercoated

FRONT END MODIFICATIONS
Shortened 2 inches

FEATURED
Easyriders, March 1996

HERITAGE FXR

The traditional fatbob gas tank look was added to the wide glide front end and old-style aluminum nacelle cowling, then the latest technology in RevTech wheels were poured into the mix.

This particular bike packs divergent elements. First, it belongs to a woman, Marcia Pence. Next, it encompasses a vastly different design direction for the FXR model.

Harley-Davidson designed the vibration-free, rubbermount drive line for the FXR series of motorcycles. The concept of rubbermounting the Harleys was stunning and promoted an immense new image. All of a sudden, the vibration was gone. FXRs also included the new Evolution engine and 5-speed transmission. Harley riders who rode rigid-mounted bikes into their 40s, suddenly felt 16 again in the saddle of the FXR.

On the other hand, the Harley Softails featured the cool Heritage models with their big retro fenders, reminiscent of the '50s bad boy image, but incorporated a harder ride and engines that were mounted directly to the frame. This basically meant that you could look cool and be uncomfortable at the same time.

Marcia Pence took it upon herself to incorporate the look of the Heritage models with the smooth ride and performance characteristics of the FXR chassis. She modified and added the heavy and wide FLH front

HERITAGE FXR

This machine was built around the Harley-Davidson, British-style performance frame for FXRs. Then the classic lines of the traditional FLH were added with large fenders.

end and the classic fenders to match. Her significant other, Peter Catherwood, designed the scooter with Arlen Ness accessories, and RevTech billet wheels. The result is cool and comfortable.

YEAR AND MAKE
1991 Harley-Davidson

OWNER
Marcia Pence

MODEL
FXLRSC

BUILDER
Peter Catherwood

ENGINE MODIFICATIONS
Dyna S single-fire ignition, Wiseco pistons, Street Heads, S&S 502 cam, Bad Dog exhaust

TRANSMISSION MODIFICATIONS
None

FINISH
Molding by Russ Foy, painting by Custom Classic, candy apple green urethane, special marble texturing

FRAME MODIFICATIONS
Swingarm modified for wide rear wheel

FRONT END MODIFICATIONS
FLH front end shortened 2 inches

FEATURED
Easyriders, December 1995

PURPLE PEOPLE EATER

Ken Moir of Fairborn, Ohio, is dedicated to this one motorcycle, and it shows in every element. Since 1987 he's rebuilt it from the ground up three different times. "It's got to the point, there's nothing else I can do," Ken said, regarding the bike, a sad, hesitant look taking over his face.

All right, so let's evaluate what he's done and grade him accordingly. Ken is a machinist and owns Ken Moir Machining. Being involved in a machine shop is perhaps the most enviable, constructive talent to have when you're custom bike building. Years ago, the best talent to have might have been welding and sheet metal fabrication, but today it's machining.

Ken took the basic design from many Arlen Ness components and fed it into his machine shop. He came up with front end, lower legs that matched the Ness design. He made his own sanitary headlight mount, caps for the bottom of his triple trees, cable guides that added detail to the frame, a billet chain guard painted to match the blurple color choice, flush-mounted axles, and a tank divider. On top of his Ness accents he retained the S&S carb cover by making it flush on the face, then adding his color scheme to it.

All right, how should we grade Ken? Whaddaya say? OK we'll give him an A+. No, wait, we don't want to pump his ego to the moon. Let's make it a C-. There, I feel better.

PURPLE PEOPLE EATER

Originally a 1982 Wide Glide, this machine has been enhanced with Ness refinements and custom touches that bring out the street custom styling without too many major modifications.

Hues of blue and purple seem to work well with chrome, and the extra highlights of the matching speedo dash and spark plug wires pull it together.

YEAR AND MAKE
1982 Harley-Davidson

OWNER
Ken Moir

MODEL
Shovelhead

BUILDER
Owner and pals

ENGINE MODIFICATIONS
Dyna S single-fire ignition, polished cases, Andrews BH grind cam, Cycle Shack exhaust, rebuilt by Red Beard, balanced by Bob's Cycle

TRANSMISSION MODIFICATIONS
Chromed case, back-cut gears

FINISH
Doug Jahnke molding and paint, blurple, special Deltron mix

FRAME MODIFICATIONS
Chromed swingarm, 5-degree rake

FRONT END MODIFICATIONS
Billet wide glide, shortened 2 inches

FEATURED
Easyriders, February 1996

THE JADE DRAGON

The engine is the centerpiece on some bikes; in this case, the paint captures the imagination and the dragons are intriguing, to say the least

"No rules" is the theme here with the paint, dragon sheet metal fabrication, frame-mounted controls, and a severe rake.

This motorcycle is all about dreams. It was originally built in 1995 for the *Easyriders* Juvenile Diabetes Foundation Sweepstakes. The concept behind the machine is one of a dragon fantasy, and it was built by two people who made their personal dreams come true.

Which of these facts should I expand on? Why make that choice when you can have it all. Pat Kennedy and his wife, Brook, have been building bikes, individually and together, for years. When the time was right, they made their move to the desert town of Tombstone, Arizona, population 1,300, and built their dream home together. They now build several award-winning bikes a year, and Brook is responsible for an entire line of 40-, 80-, and 120-spoke wheels. All right, so that's their dream, and it became an everyday reality.

Pat created the Dragon fantasy for the sweepstakes to catch the imagination of young and old alike, and he more than succeeded in capturing its spirit with this righteous wizard's ride.

The final dream involved the sweepstakes itself. Five bikes were built, and the lucky winner was able to choose his favorite from among the masterful machines.

YEAR AND MAKE
1995 Harley-Davidson

OWNER
Pat Kennedy

MODEL
Pat Kennedy Custom

BUILDER
Pat Kennedy

ENGINE MODIFICATIONS
S&S lower end, Arias pistons, STD cases, Xzotic Pan rocker covers, Leineweber cam, Pat Kennedy exhaust, Keihin carburetor

TRANSMISSION MODIFICATIONS
Polished case, Andrews gears, 66-tooth wheel sprocket

FINISH
Molding by Pat Kennedy, painted by Darrell Pinney, Jade paint by Deltron, airbrush art by Darrell Pinney

FRAME MODIFICATIONS
Pat Kennedy Softail frame, 35-degree rake, 2-inch stretch, struts incorporated into rear fender

FRONT END MODIFICATIONS
Pat Kennedy adjustable forks, 6 inches over stock, fully adjustable

FEATURED
Easyriders, November 1995

A BLUR AND A HOWL

This machine captures clean lines with a whole new textured approach and smeared flamed treatment, as if the rider had slammed into a paint truck.

This is a tale of passion trading place with routine. Joe Chavez owns Billet Concepts, an aftermarket custom components billet manufacturer. Before he found his way into the two-wheeled industry, he was a manufacturer of aerospace components. Joe worked so that he could indulge in his true passion—his motorcycle.

He rode to escape the rigors of work, society, and restrictions. Just about the time he built a successful entity, the aerospace industry faded. Joe was left with a couple of million dollars' worth of machinery and not a damn order to fill.

Now he rode out of desperation, wondering what his next move would be. He became a regular at all the local watering holes, and one night while drowning his sorrows, the rider next to him said: "Say, Joe. It's none of my business, but why don't you stop crying. It's embarrassing. Why don't you go back to the shop right now and develop a stronger aluminum? Call it 7075 and make it ten times stronger than 6061. While you're at it, make some forward controls, a brake pedal and gearshift, some mirrors, grips, and pegs. Then you might as well fabricate a master cylinder, hydraulic clutch cylinder, some risers, and trick trees for that hunk of junk you're riding."

Joe looked up at his neighbor and with a bar napkin wiped his eyes.

A BLUR AND A HOWL

Gas tanks have become works of art. This one flows to a distinct point and incorporates a contoured gas cap to make it ultra-clean.

With new technology available, the rear of a Daytec custom frame begins to look this clean, coupled with a Performance Machine wheel and matching rotor.

He didn't know what to say and just stared at the figure in the shadows on the corner stool.

"Don't say a word, Joe. Just get off your ass and get out of here."

Joe heeded the advice, and Billet Concepts was born.

YEAR AND MAKE
1995 Harley-Davidson

OWNER
Joe Chavez

MODEL
Billet Concept

BUILDER
Billet Concepts

ENGINE MODIFICATIONS
S&S 93-cubic-inch lower end, J&E pistons, Delkron cases, Performance Techniques heads, Headquarters cam, Dell 'Orto carburetor, Siamese Drag pipes, Dyna ignition

TRANSMISSION MODIFICATIONS
Andrews gears, 70-tooth wheel sprocket, 32-tooth trans sprocket

FINISH
Painted by Damon's, red, silver pearl, black urethane, marbleized by Damon's

FRAME MODIFICATIONS
Daytec chassis, Softail wide drive, 2-degree rake, 2-inch stretch

FRONT END MODIFICATIONS
41mm mid glide, Billet Concepts custom trees

FEATURED
Easyriders, November 1995

TEMPTING FATE

Ron Simms and crew form the Bay Area Custom Cycles organization. This particular bike demonstrates how they made the final adjustments to a Softail, insuring the righteous rigid look. Ron and his staff hid the fender struts inside the swingarm so as not to interfere with the line of the frame. In addition, they didn't replace the swingarm with a billet monster, or chrome the original, or change the color of the swingarm away from the frame's theme.

Following Ron's righteous and true, never-say-die, rockin' style, this bike follows the code of classic Simms' customizing with the wide rear tire, shortened front end, exquisitely detailed engine, and a series of signature Simms accessories, including all the lightning bolt parts. Add legendary paint by Horst, and you have the Bay Area Custom Cycle look at its best.

One of the keys to Ron's success is his ability to build iron-fisted, reliable machines. His bikes are ridden regularly and usually with impunity. In other words, they're bulletproof! For Ron, it's not enough to have the best-looking bikes in town—they've got to be the toughest and fastest.

Embroidered on the back of each of his jackets is the slogan: "Till The End." Ron means every word, damn it.

TEMPTING FATE

Ron Simms knows how to make the rear of his bikes consistent with the overall design through wide, low-profile tires, widened fenders, and hidden fender rails.

Tough-looking choppers start several ways, but the most obvious is with high bars that give any motorcycle an unruly appearance. The higher, the more outlandish and daring.

YEAR AND MAKE
1995 Harley-Davidson

OWNER
Ron Simms

MODEL
Simms Custom Softail

BUILDER
The crew at
Bay Area Custom Cycles

ENGINE MODIFICATIONS
S&S 89-cubic-inch engine, Dyna S ignition, STD and Hannan's heads, Thunder Header exhaust

TRANSMISSION MODIFICATIONS
Simms shifting

FINISH
Paint and molding by Horst, green and black urethane, House of Kolor special paint

FRAME MODIFICATIONS
Paughco/Simms chassis, 5-degree rake, hidden fender rails

FRONT END MODIFICATIONS
Paughco springer, 2 inches under stock

FEATURED
Easyriders, October 1995

SOMETHING OLD, SOMETHING NEW

A basket case, this economically detailed machine was built from bits and pieces of other bikes and eras. Also known as a swap meet special, it has budget style.

Mil Blair has been in the custom motorcycle business since 1959. That year was a banner one for Mil. He escaped reform school and the shivering winters of Minnesota and rode his mid-'40s Knucklehead to the warm beaches of Santa Monica, California. That same year he started a business making fine parts for custom Harleys.

As the years passed, he built a major custom bike distribution business (Jammer), assisted with the start of *Easyriders* magazine, and continued to build bikes. He's created more than 100 bikes over the last 40 years, and is still running strong. You can imagine the number of parts ol' Mil has accumulated over the years, and the various styles and trends the custom industry had peeled through. So when he decided to build this little pavement pounder, all he had to do was stumble into his garage and trip over one initial part, which was a prototype Paughco frame with a stock rake angle.

Setting the frame on his lift, he turned on the single dangling bulb in the dark mass of crumpled boxes and milk crates. The illumination fanned out over a myriad of rusting and chipped components from the last three and a half decades. A pair of tarnished spun aluminum wheels stuck out from a box of old Jammer parts. He pulled them free and discovered some early Performance Machine disc brake components.

So it went into the night, scrambling from box to crate, drawer to drooping shelf, until he had the makings of something entirely different from his creative past.

Keeping the chrome and polishing bills to a minimum, Mil Blair combined black wheels with bolt-on accessories and a flat fender to cover the tough road warrior image.

Everything flows with black, chrome, and an aggregate of small, tucked-in components such as the nominal turn signals, low seat, and minimum mirrors to keep it bad and simple.

YEAR AND MAKE
1994 Blair Special Construction

OWNER
Mil Blair

MODEL
Black and Chrome

BUILDER
Owner

ENGINE MODIFICATIONS
Crane ignition, 95-inch S&S lower end, Sputhe pistons, STD cases, Leineweber S5 cam, S&S carburetor, Custom Chrome exhaust

TRANSMISSION MODIFICATIONS
Bits and pieces

FINISH
Painted by Jim Torre, very black Deltron paint

FRAME MODIFICATIONS
Paughco chassis with 30-degree rake

FRONT END MODIFICATIONS
Frank's tubes, 2 inches under, Drag Specialities trees

FEATURED
Easyriders, June 1995

FIREBALL FXR

The Corbin Warbird fiberglass kit transforms a stock Harley-Davidson into an instant road racing legend. Performance Machine billet aluminum brakes, rotors, and wheels set it off.

There are only a few names you will see repeated throughout this book: Harley-Davidson, S&S, and Performance Machine. What do these three have in common? They all share a dedication to design, quality, fit, and function. That formula particularly applies to Perry Sands and his company Performance Machine, the premier custom wheel and brake manufacturer in the motorcycle industry.

The custom bike world is a constantly changing arena. In the beginning there was the bobbed Harley, then the chopper, then super-stretched monster bikes appeared, then the Arlen Ness style, etc. In the '80s and '90s riders and builders all over the country questioned what would be next. Bikes got lower and

Chrome, polished aluminum, and red paint cut the number of finishes and colors on the bike to three, enhancing its tight appearance.

leeker, retro looks such as Indian-tyled fenders returned, and the ustoms got wilder and more futuristic. ut deep inside a bottle of Cuervo old is an insidious worm of vast and allucinogenic powers. Once ingested, he worm often produces downright trange effects in bike builders.

It may have been during one such sychedelic session that premier custom seat manufacturer Mike Corbin created the WWII fighter plane-inspired War Bird seen here. Mike went forth, preaching the word of ultra-fast, V-twin sport-bikes and wild styling.

Perry Sands heard the word and was bitten by the bug... or, should that be, bitten by the demon-like hallucinogenic worm?

YEAR AND MAKE
1991 Harley-Davidson

OWNER
Perry Sands

MODEL
War Bird

BUILDER
Performance Machine

ENGINE MODIFICATIONS
88-cubic-inch Carl's Speed Shop motor, points ignition, Axtell 9.5:1 C.R. pistons, Carl's True Flow heads, Carl's CM 580 Lift Cam, S&S carburetor, Bub Bad Dog exhaust

TRANSMISSION MODIFICATIONS
Polished and dressed

FINISH
Molded and painted by Damon's, Damon's red paint

FRAME MODIFICATIONS
Performance Machine wide fender kit

FRONT END MODIFICATIONS
Polished and chromed narrow glide

FEATURED
Easyriders, March 1995

BOUND BY HONOR

Hector used a proliferation of Arlen Ness slotted billet components to bring the bike to life, then rechromed everything for a consistent finish

The difference between Hector's bikes and the average custom, and one of the reasons his bike was chosen to appear on these pages, involves his extreme attention to detail. That's not to say the bike lacks design or creativity, which is clearly not the case, but the overwhelmingly striking aspect of this bike is its cleanliness and detail.

Did you know that all chrome is not the same? It's not particularly noticeable until you place several examples of chrome parts together under a light and inspect them. You'll discover that some chrome has a yellow cast, and some has a darker cast as if it's tinted (environmental concerns often affect the quality of chrome). So what does Hector do? He rechromes absolutely everything and makes sure that the chromer understands that all the chrome is to be of the highest, brightest quality.

Hector also insists on a minimum of metal finishes on his bike. If a builder uses the chrome he gets from various manufacturers, plus polished parts, plus bead-blasted parts, plus some stainless steel, it's like painting everything slightly different colors. It may not make a big difference overall, but when it comes to inspecting the detail, the results definitely show.

Look closely at this machine.

BOUND BY HONOR

The key to Hector Sedano's customs is cleanliness and simplicity of design. There isn't better detailed engine in this book.

Hector went right out of his way to insure a minimum of variation. And he extends a similar philosophy to his paint schemes. To sum things up: keep it clean and simple, and the bike will take on a sanitary and unified appearance.

YEAR AND MAKE
1994 Harley-Davidson

OWNER
Hector Sedano

MODEL
Wide Drive

BUILDER
Owner, Doran Benson

ENGINE MODIFICATIONS
98-cubic-inch S&S stroker built by Westside Custom Cycles, electronic ignition, S&S pistons, Dell 'Orto dual-throat carburetor, nitrous system

TRANSMISSION MODIFICATIONS
Chromed case, Pro-One wheel sprocket

FINISH
Molding and painting by Bryan Kinney, white with blue pearl Cronar paint, illustrations by Ken Michaelsen

FRAME MODIFICATIONS
Pro Atlas chassis, slammed, 35-degree rake

FRONT END MODIFICATIONS
Billet, chromed trees, lowers turned and chromed

FEATURED
Easyriders, July 1995

DOWNSIZING DYNAS

The rule of the '90s is stretched tanks, contoured to enhance the profile of the motorcycle, fit the seat and flow into the top of the frame. It's the one rule to follow.

Bob McKay of McKay's Custom Creations in Shallow Lake, Ontario, Canada, built this Dyna Super Glide to fit his 5-foot-tall wife, Dianne. In addition, this is a true street custom, with a mostly unaltered frame and only a brief number of accessories to bring it to life.

Most of the components on this bike originated from the Custom Chrome catalog. Bob modified and radiused the fenders himself and stretched the gas tanks to fit the frame. After 25 years of bike building, he still enjoys the challenge of fitting a bike to the customer. I gotta tell you, though, it's much easier and more eye-appealing to build a bike for someone 4 feet tall than it is to build a bike for someone cresting 7 feet.

Lower shocks are available to drop the rear, and kits to chop down a front end are only a catalog away. Many builders rake necks to drop the bike even farther. Short handlebars are available from any number of sources; adjusted kickstands are easy

Dyna Glides are the latest frame style for Harley-Davidsons. It takes a couple of years before the custom market gets used to the lines.

enough to order by phone. Demoted bikes seem compact and condensed. They also look sleeker, tougher and wider, and the engine looks even bigger. But building a long bike that fits a tall drink of water like yours truly presents an even tougher challenge. I wonder if Bob's up to it.

YEAR AND MAKE
1995 Harley-Davidson

OWNER
Bob McKay

MODEL
Dyna Glide

BUILDER
McKay's Custom Creations

ENGINE MODIFICATIONS
Dyna 2000 ignition, flat top pistons, Headquarters heads, Headquarters 600 lift cam, constant velocity carb, 2-inch Samson exhaust

TRANSMISSION MODIFICATIONS
Blueprinted

FINISH
Painted and molded by Bob McKay, organic green House of Kolor paint, layered graphics

FRAME MODIFICATIONS
Smoothed and raked to 33 degrees

FRONT END MODIFICATIONS
Progressive Suspension springs, lowered 3 inches

FEATURED
Easyriders, December 1995

NOT OF THIS WORLD

This bike pays homage to the H.R. Giger creations from the movie Alien. *The owner built this monster and a cathedral to all that drives a man to obscene art.*

I have written of dedication before on these pages, of the torrent of creativity, a fearsome passion that storms from a man's soul as he attempts to bring his beast to life.

Bryan Bajakian's foray into the deep recesses of H.R. Giger's creature design in *Alien* began as a collaborative effort with a bike, some leather, and an airbrush artist named Kram. Kram illustrated the ghastly figures, then Bryan rendered these eerie works of Giger with the help of a local stainless steel sculptor who worked from clay molds. The team's first fait accompli was the gargoyle's head, spouting a torrent of fiery passion, pulsating through eyes and a mouth that serve as the taillight.

Bryan's gnarled and twisted vision continued to reveal itself in the Softail dash, which is composed of 75 human and inhuman creature heads. Imagine the time and detail involved and the stress placed on a mere mortal. The project lagged, or Bryan became so obsessed with covering the entire motorcycle in demons that his demands drove his cohorts to leave town. Bryan was finally forced to take over the roll of clay sculptor.

For three long years Bryan became a recluse in a dank cave while he churned out increasingly detailed images of Giger-esque grotesqueries, taking on far more intricate detail than the artist suggested in his one-dimensional paintings. Bryan is an example of what happens to a man possessed with the desire to bring a Harley to life in a likeness that is not of this world. God help us all.

NOT OF THIS WORLD

The tanks, although original in shape, contain a dash panel inlaid with more than 75 human body parts and creature heads.

Here's the first piece concocted by the doctor to initiate a three-year project: The taillight was hand-sculpted then molded and cast to bring the beast to life.

YEAR AND MAKE
1990 Harley-Davidson

OWNER
Bryan Bajakian

MODEL
Monster FLSTF

BUILDER
Owner

ENGINE MODIFICATIONS
Screamin' Eagle ignition, polished cases, ported and polished heads, Screamin' Eagle Stage 2 cam, S&S Super E carburetor, Cycle Shack with sculptured exhaust, sculpted air cleaner

TRANSMISSION MODIFICATIONS
Cases polished by owner

FINISH
Spoiler by Kram, molding and paint by Kram, shades of steel lacquer base with urethane top, all special paint by Kram

FRAME MODIFICATIONS
Chassis molded in steel by owner

FRONT END MODIFICATIONS
All chrome

FEATURED
Easyriders, December 1995

LOW BRO

This road racing Harley sports Performance Machine brakes and Boyd's wheels, but the amber windshield, the goofy fenders, and the yellow seats take it to a winding mountain race.

Here we go again. That creative urge runs rampant in our motorcycles. Just about the time the pot is simmering, someone tosses in a dash of cayenne pepper and the damn thing boils over.

In this case, the racing family of the White Brothers, Tom and Dan, who have earned a major role in the custom and race parts distributor arena with their 20-year-old southern California business, built a motorcycle to showcase their talents.

With the assistance of Denny Berg of Time Machine in Huntington Beach, California, Tom and Dan reached into their past, into their catalog, and into the essence of the Harley mystique to design the bike you see on these pages.

"We incorporated the rear frame design from a British BSA Gold Star and combined it with the characteristic '50-style Harley look of a short, narrow dirttracker fender, solo seat, and pillion pad to totally

The air cleaner cover as a work of metal-shaping art. The windshield was added to the traditional headlight nacelle, though the cowling is painted to match the bike's theme.

disguise the rear end," said Tom. "The FL front headlight was retained so that nobody could mistake the bike's Harley heritage, and we threw in the windscreen for fun."

The plan included avoiding chrome and numerous accessories. Sometimes the best-looking bikes have little in the way of flash, sport fewer accessories, and promote a simplistic theme. The brothers have accomplished the ultimate tribute to their business in this eyeball-popping, one-of-a-kind ride.

YEAR AND MAKE
1990 Harley-Davidson

OWNER
White Brothers

MODEL
Bros. FLST

BUILDER
Denny Berg, Time Machine

ENGINE MODIFICATIONS
10:1 Wiseco pistons, Patrick Racing heads, Crane 1101 cam, Mikuni HSR 42 carburetor, White Bros. 2-into-1 exhaust, balancing by Denny Berg

TRANSMISSION MODIFICATIONS
Blueprinted, UMI controls, HES offset gears

FINISH
Molding by Denny Berg, painting by Ray Newton, Molly Graphics, blended yellow, special paint by the Wizard

FRAME MODIFICATIONS
33-degree rake, shaved rails, hidden wiring, metal wrapped

FRONT END MODIFICATIONS
White Power by White Bros. inverted forks, 2 inches under, adjustable upside-down aluminum trees

FEATURED
Easyriders, January 1995

CLASSIC & TOURERS

ALTHOUGH THESE TWO BIKES ARE FEATURED IN THE SAME CHAPTER THEY ARE OFTEN FOUND AT OPPOSITE ENDS OF THE SPECTRUM

Hang on for this one. Although classics and touring bikes, or dressers as we still call them affectionately, seem to fit the same mold, the governing point being appearance, that's sometimes as far as the similarities go. They appear akin because of the stock configuration, but they're opposites. They actually represent two biker planets: the absolutely most reliable, functional bikes and the oldest, most outdated, most likely to break down. I'll get drawn and quartered for that last comment, but by today's standards, whatever that means, it's fact. Well, hell, you wouldn't ride a 1923 J model to Sturgis. All right, so I would, but I'd also put aside a month to get there.

Okay, I'll say it. I enjoy working on classic bikes. They're less complex, the parts fit ... generally. Touring bikes also primarily use stock components, so construction takes less engineering, and there are fewer one-of-a-kind components to deal with.

A "custom touring bike" is in some respects an oxymoron. Touring indicates a large assortment of bells and whistles, creature comforts and added accessories. Generally, the mad customizer is looking for items to remove from his project to form it into the custom of his nightmares. That's directly in contrast to the notion of touring.

So where did we go wrong? It goes largely part and parcel with the American spirit. One of the notorious Codes Of The West, code number 12, section 2, clearly states, "Change everything. Make it individual. Make it wild. Above all, say NO to stock." In other words, no matter how reliable the original is, take it apart, chrome it (so it won't fit anymore), bondo everything, change the frame geometry, and take off anything that disturbs the line of the bike. In effect, almost take the tour out of touring!

Now, don't get me wrong. I'm not discussing a garbage barge, complete with enough headlights to lead a parade, every accessory on the market, and a barbecue on the tour pack. I don't consider those bikes customs; they're more like collections.

On the other hand, the classic is just that—a slightly modified original from an era with class. That era designation can be based on my preemptors, the time you were born, etc. I say that anything earlier than 1958 is a true classic. Older guys would disagree with this; younger guys don't care. Actually, a classic is in the eyes of the beholder or the builder. Hell, some riders think Vespas are classics. That's how jaded the world has become. My personal definition includes all the rigid-framed Harleys. Some might say all the Panheads until the advent of the Shovel in 1966. Others might go for anything older than the cone motor in 1970. And some would kick my ass for embracing anything newer than the beginning of the overhead valve Knucklehead in 1936.

It's confusing and wonderful at the same time. Classics are the biker's heritage, and they represent the foundation on which the industry is built today. Besides, they're cool.

BLACK ATTACK

The rear of the bike is low and the short Progressive Suspension shocks make it even lower.

We coupled touring bikes such as this one with classics due to styling similarities. Originally, this bike appeared in the pages of *Easyriders* because of its traditional lines and interesting combination of touring attributes mixed with custom accessories. Arlen Ness was one of the first radical builders who blended choppers with touring, probably because he was logging as many miles as most dresser riders.

Arlen took old cop bikes and created a line of Luxury Liners based on his chromed creed: "Say No To Stock." Ness found that longer riding distances and long open roads demanded more storage space and a more comfortable seating position than could be afforded on a custom chopper. But how do you blend long range comfort with a heavy dose of style?

Enter Tom Motzko, the Purchasing Director for Drag Specialties, one of the top three custom motorcycle distributors in America. Tom has unlimited access to an ever-widening line of parts for Harleys, but in this case he specifically built this bike on a carefully outlined and followed budget.

The Harley FXRP entered Tom's life used and broken. He lowered the seat height 1 1/5 inches to fit his diminutive frame, stretched the overall length of the bike, brought it closer to the ground with shorter Progressive Suspension shocks, and

BLACK ATTACK

The front fairing establishes the bike as a touring machine with a heavy guarded front and charcoal windshield.

The Tom Motzko, Drag Specialties "Black Attack" couples sleek styling with touring lines. It combines looks and function for the best of all worlds.

lengthened the look of the bike with Ness tail-dragger fenders, then blacked most of the machine.

Arlen Ness may have created this style of custom bike that can haul the toughest bikers across country comfortably and without feeling that they're riding a bone-stock, fresh-out-of-the-crate touring tuna boat, but Tom took Arlen's theme and pumped his own style of class and charisma into it. Although the pictures don't depict it, the bike was set up to mount two very large saddlebags to the rear fender rails, making this the limousine of touring customs.

Imagine rolling into a small Midwestern town, 600 miles from nowhere, to refuel. The rider is adorned in all black leathers and a full faced, gloss-black helmet. His face shield is tinted black so outsiders are not afforded the opportunity to peer into his eyes. He dismounts as a gangly young kid stumbles out of the back of the garage to find the phantom rider pumping fuel into his rocket ship.

Black Attack

The inside of the fairing has been carefully detailed and the Drag Specialties handlebars don't interfere with the bike's sloping appearance.

The sweating, greasy-palmed teen stands in the blistering sun and watches the masked rider fill his tank in silence. For a moment in time, everything is still. The kid doesn't move as his brain fills with the image of the black rider and his shimmering ebony machine contrasting with the sun-washed surroundings. In the blink of an eye, the kid's mouth drops open, a soiled rag slips from his hand, and his life changes forever.

He will never again accept mediocrity in his life. Color and chrome with change his existence for all time. Nothing bland will do. As he watches the rider mount his steed and the scream of the exhaust system shatters the silence, he flies headlong into the realization that his life has somehow been altered. Even the sound the machine makes breaks all semblance of the status quo. The sleek motorcycle and its rider reek of color, contrast, style, and living life to the fullest. The rear wheel spins, throwing a rooster tail of dust and sand back at the rusting station as the lone rider disappears around the bend ahead.

BLACK ATTACK

The Don's Custom Cycle paint job pulls the entire piece together with level graphics designed by Dawber that connect all the elements.

YEAR AND MAKE
1990 Harley-Davidson

OWNER
Tom Motzko

MODEL
FXRP

BUILDER
Owner, Mun, Donnie

ENGINE MODIFICATIONS
Engine rebuilt by Eagle Engineering, Crane/ACCEL ignition, Drag Specialties pistons, ported heads, Crane 1103 cam, S&S E carburetor, Samson/RunRoader exhaust, JIMS lifters

TRANSMISSION MODIFICATIONS
Andrews gears, Landmark Manufacturing shift linkage

FINISH
Molding and paint by Don's Custom Cycle, black with peach sherbet mint green graphics, special paint designed by Dawber

FRAME MODIFICATIONS
Chassis built by Ness, H-D, and Bob Munroe, swingarm by Donnie Smith, 3-inch stretch, Progressive Suspension shocks

FRONT END MODIFICATIONS
39 mm H-D forks, 2 inches under stock, Ness conversion, Progressive Suspension springs

FEATURED
Easyriders, July 1995

Drag Specialties classical wire wheels tied with quality GMA billet aluminum disc brakes that have been powdercoated to keep the theme intact.

BLUE COLLAR BEHEMOTH

Mike Crawford, the builder, kept the profile of this touring model completely tight by not having anything stick out or above the designed lines of the machine. There are no windshields, no antennas, no sissybars, no passenger seats, no tall mirrors ... no way.

This scoot began its illustrious life as a police motorcycle, which ultimately was retired to the private sector when current owner Jerry "Kraut" Davis purchased it. Originally Jerry's mission statement contained only one precept: to paint it and ride. But as we've discovered, that is rarely the case. Jerry decided on basic black as the color for his ride. Then he met with master customizer Mike Crawford, who explained how he could inject classic lines by simply tearing the bike to the ground, raking the frame, and shifting the position of the rear suspension to lower the overall chassis. Jerry nodded in suspended belief, and they went to work. Jerry had his doubts.

With the frame modified and the wheels and front end in place, the two men stood back and Mike's evangelistic Southern voice summoned the gods of chrome. Jerry testified and the sizzling service began. As the fervor grew, Mike the preacher professed that they had accomplished more than they had set out to do, but they were still far from the promised land. In flowery tones he proclaimed that with recessed rear lights, cut-down handlebars, chopped fenders, a hand-formed aluminum frame shroud, custom fender rail covers, and filler strips between the bags and the rear fender, they might just reach their goal.

Say Harley-lujah!

"We cut the gas tank and inserted a piece of three-inch pipe, so the speedo cable could run through it," said Jerry. "Then we made a door that lifts up out of the dash's centerpiece and put the gas cap

underneath." While the engine was being carefully rebuilt by Bruce Blevins, they refinished the exterior of the entire driveline to reflect black with a few chrome highlights.

During the frame trans-formation, the front end was removed and Mike proclaimed the need to modify the forks and the shrouds to flow into the lines of the rest of the bike. The entire front end accessory package was then polished and painted to match the rest of the bike.

Finally, the day came when the unworthy disciple of custom creations stood back to admire his finished work. A touring bike had been converted from a heathen of the streets to a sleek, classic touring machine ready to flow like the wind. It had become a machine the god of chrome would be proud to own, and to ride from one end of the galaxy to the other. And so it was on the final day of creation—the bros went for beers.

The black theme continues with the black horn, primaries, dash panel, riser cap, and controls. Small judicious touches of chrome highlight the machine.

BLUE COLLAR BEHEMOTH

Touring bikes afford builders new ways to go in the custom world. Check the rear section of this bike and the recessed turn signals, the LED taillight, the blacked-out paint scheme, and the turned-out mufflers.

YEAR AND MAKE
1991 H-D

OWNER
Jerry Davis

MODEL
FLHTP

ENGINE MODIFICATIONS
Rebuilt by Bruce Blevins, electronic ignition, Police special 80-cubic-inch engine, CV carburetor, S&S pushrods and air cleaner

TRANSMISSION MODIFICATIONS
None

FINISH
Molding by owner, paint by Tim Hines, black PPG urethane, graphics by Darin

FRAME MODIFICATIONS
Modified by Mike Crawford, 35-degree rake, relocated shocks

FRONT END MODIFICATIONS
Wide glide forks, painted black

FEATURED
Easyriders, April 1996

The front end received a similar all-black treatment with painted lower legs, covers, cowling, fender, and brake caliper. Only the headlight rim and Sturgis wheel remains polished or chromed.

DRAGGIN' TAIL

Aside from the S&S carburetor cover every auxiliary bauble is stock Harley-Davidson. Note the lavishly extensive battery covers and engine covers.

George Donaldson has created the ultimate classic-style touring model in this Shovelhead. "I grew up in the fifties," said George, sipping a draft at the pub. "Bikes that looked like this are what I saw as a kid." So George got himself a ratty 1979 FLH and tore into it.

In 1979 this bike represented the state-of-the-art Harley touring motorcycle, fully accessorized. Although no 1979 FLH looked as good as this one does. George rechromed everything. His chroming bill must have gone through the roof. "I put seventy hours in molding the frame alone," he said. George extended the rear fender 7 inches and lowered the bike 3 inches. Then he covered the perfectly finished frame with every custom 1979 FLH part known to man. But just before he installed each chrome doodad, he painted the inside white pearl.

This guy's a fanatic, and his slammed scoot carries a good lesson about staying brutally true to the theme of the bike, with even the most minute details. He wanted the sucker ultra low from stem to stern. He even chopped the mirror stems to make the sideview mirrors set low and close to the bars. Then he searched for lower bars and replaced the originals with a set of low-style police issue handlebars.

The wide glide front end is adorned with every stainless steel accessory and chromed doodad imaginable.

And he refused to run a windshield for fear it would make the bike pop up in the front.

Finally, while searching an obscure dealership for additional accessories for his rolling shrimp boat, he discovered a white-fringed seat collecting dust on a back shelf. When he brought it to the clerk's attention, the little spud behind the counter began to howl. "It's not for sale—it's just a conversation piece," the salesman said, rolling on the floor. "Who the hell would want to run a white fringed seat?"

"I'll take it," George said and hauled the stylish solo home along with a set of white grips and footboards to match. Of course, all the white and extra paint don't necessarily fit with the touring theme of the bike, but neither does a configuration that can't clear a pack of cigarettes without scraping the long fishtail pipes. Most touring freaks prefer windshields to catch the myriad of bugs hovering above open highways. But what the hell, cool is where it's at.

George has been riding dressers for a decade, and perhaps he has no intentions of riding this low boy across the country. On the other hand, if he did want to escape a dead end job or a dead girlfriend, there's nothing stopping him from riding this bike anywhere—not even giggling truck drivers who spy the flapping fringe, forest rangers trying to curtail his rooster tail of sparks, or the girl's revenge-seeking relatives. So, go for it, George.

HARLEY-DAVIDSON
HARLEY-DAVIDSON 
S&S
SUPER

The white fringed seat was an original accessory that was rarely used due to the fragile nature of its appearance, not to mention cleaning chores. The dash has been chromed and an accessory shroud added.

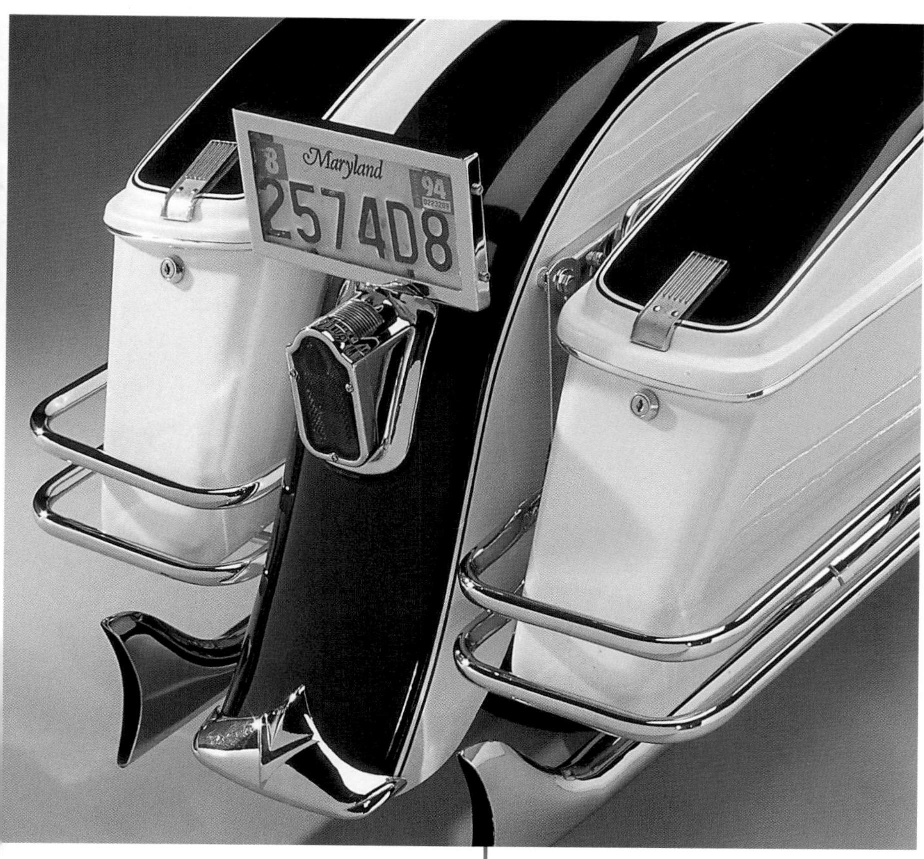

Even the front brake covers, shifter covers, mud guards and amber running lights were added to this rolling gee-gaw package.

Classic fiberglass saddlebags with all the trim including protective rails and a custom license plate frame. Note extras like the fishtail exhaust and chromed taillight.

YEAR AND MAKE
1979 Harley-Davidson

OWNER
George Donaldson

MODEL
FLH

BUILDER
American Cycle Performance

ENGINE MODIFICATIONS
80-cubic-inch engine rebuilt by American Cycle Performance, Crane ignition, Custom Chrome pistons, pocket ported heads, S&S Shorty carburetor, fishtail exhaust

TRANSMISSION MODIFICATIONS
23-tooth tranny sprocket, 51-tooth rear wheel sprocket

FINISH
Molded and painted by owner, pearl white and radiance purple, special paint by George

FRONT END MODIFICATIONS
Stock FLH, lowered 2 inches, polished lower legs

FORKS MODIFICATIONS
lowered 2 inches, custom fork caps

FEATURED
Easyriders, January 1995

DEEP BLUE

The running lights in the front and rear were gleaned from archival truck parts and massaged to fit and function with the classic.

For a couple of decades, custom motorcycles were made from bits and pieces of everything, from old doorknobs for shifters, to chunks of wood replacing the stock dash panels. It wasn't a matter of computer illustrations and programmable milling machines. It took a wild imagination, a torch, and lots of time to make unique components.

Kent Kozera's Flathead is a perfect example. He drives a 1959 chopped Caddy Coupe with deep purple ghost flames, and this classic two-wheeler echoes the look and feel of his too-cool Coupe to a tee. Galen Olsen, the fabricator and long, longtime bike builder, hired on to bring the scoot back to life the old fashioned way. Galen dug through his garage to uncover his stash of old automotive and bike lights and found a set of 1937 Dodge tail lamps to replace the factory spotlights.

Galen mated a pair of 1954 Ford truck lenses to the taillights, and front turn signals from a 1940 Chevy were recruited for the rear running lights. Then Galen split a '39 Packard headlamp shell lengthwise and fabricated an unusually shaped air cleaner for the big Flathead. The only off-the-shelf part used on this machine was an old set of Flanders, brass risers to lift the black handlebars.

A stock replacement muffler restricted the sound of the mighty 82-inch side valve. They experimented with a megaphone muffler with a fish tip welded on—still not right. Finally, Kent and Galen fabricated a muffler for performance and pavement-slapping sound. This is how it was done in the past, a time when every component carried a sense of accomplishment. Ride on.

DEEP BLUE

A 1942 Flathead Harley-Davidson, this bike couples the original elements of its era with car parts and chopper styling.

Paint was used judiciously to cause the lines of the bike to flow, forming a cohesive theme.

YEAR AND MAKE
1942 Harley-Davidson

OWNER
Kent Kozera

MODEL
ULH

BUILDER
Owner, Galen Olsen

ENGINE MODIFICATIONS
82 cubic inches, special finned aluminum heads, #4 H-D cam, Linkert carburetor, hand-fabricated muffler and air cleaner

TRANSMISSION MODIFICATIONS
Full box of Andrews gears

FINISH
Molding and paint by Dale Kelly, black purple urethane, special ghost flames

FRAME MODIFICATIONS
Cleaned-up

FRONT END MODIFICATIONS
Galen Olsen rebuilt and filled, custom spotlights

FEATURED
Easyriders, September 1995

ONE TRICK PONY

This motorcycle represents old time classic Harley-Davidson design, coupling the latest technology with classic styling.

This machine represents the best of the old and the new combined to afford owner and Texas rancher Mark Norman the reliability of today's Harleys coupled with yesterday's style. The Heritage Softail was designed to capture the legacy of the '50s rigid frame look, but Paragon Locomotion of Deerfield Beach, Florida, took this scooter back even further and made it reminiscent of a 1936 Knucklehead.

All right, so this bike has about twice the class and chrome as any '36, but the boys at Paragon did a helluva job of replacing new components with parts from the Knuck era. This can be seen in details such as the mufflers, dash, flex tubing over the pipes, old-style horn, luggage rack, beehive taillight, old-style oil filter and lines, and Jiffy center stand. They went the opposite direction with some of the new components such as hiding the disc brake master cylinder, which is usually strapped onto the bars.

The crew at Paragon worked with Mark on 200-year-old Native

The saddle and the paint work as a tribute to the culture and talents of native American Indians. The colors and the conchos on the seat blend the old west with this '90s horse.

American Indian touches such as the buckskin elk hide leather seat adorned with 40 classic silver conchos, and paint graphics taken from Texas Indian heritage. Even the earth tones selected for the paint scheme are a tribute to the men who roamed the Texas plains long before motorcycles.

This is classic Harley-Davidson, borne of the present and reminiscent of a style that will never grow old.

YEAR AND MAKE
1994 Harley-Davidson

OWNER
Mark Norman

MODEL
Springer Softail

BUILDER
Paragon Locomotion

ENGINE MODIFICATIONS
Screamin' Eagle ignition, Ted's heads (ported and polished), Crane cam, Screamin' Eagle carburetor, Paragon Locomotion exhaust, Custom Chrome air cleaner, Antique Cycle muffler

TRANSMISSION MODIFICATIONS
None

FINISH
Molding and painting by Paragon Locomotion, red, orange candy urethane, special paint by Paragon Locomotion

FRAME MODIFICATIONS
33-degree rake, swingarm widened

FRONT END MODIFICATIONS
Stock springer shortened 2 inches

FEATURED
Easyriders, January 1996

CHAMPION PAN

Here's the most acceptable custom in the book. Perhaps the most gaudy, but still, every accessory on this machine was blessed by the factory in Milwaukee, Wisconsin.

The gentleman who owns this accessorized 1956 Panhead (1948-1965) may look normal, but deep down he's a classic maniacal, compulsive/obsessive case, much the same as many of the other builders featured in this book.

It took Bill Huykman 10 years to finish fully accessorizing this restoration. The bike has every chromed bauble available to this model in 1956. It has so many trinkets we had to classify it as a custom.

Get this—the decade-long restoration took place entirely in the man's living room. Each year as the holiday season approached, rather than relegate the prized Pan to the garage and haul in the Yuletide pine tree, he strapped decorative lights and balls to the bike and it stayed implanted in the house.

Back in 1956 a new dealership in Chillicothe, Ohio, sold the Panhead to a rider for parade duty. It was ridden regularly with a sidecar until 1962 when the owner was unfairly ticketed and he parked the classic in his back yard for 24 long years. "That'll show 'em," he thought.

Those who attempted to purchase the bike were summarily asked to leave. It was only when the local dealer offered to trade a mint condition 1978 Shovelhead dresser straight across for the weathered antique that he relented. Bill snatched up the Panhead immediately, swearing that he would never ride it until the bike was adorned with every gewgaw or talisman available in the 1956 catalog.

Bikers are nuts.

CHAMPION PAN

You can study this bike for hours, challenging your ability to spot every accessory, like the small chromed spark plug canister, the ring of lights on the wheels, the air pump, the extra chevrons, the speedo cowling, the lamented shift knob, the fender skirts and rails, and the exhaust shields. You take it from here.

YEAR AND MAKE
1956 Harley-Davidson

OWNER
Bill Huykman

MODEL
FLH (one of 224)

BUILDER
Bill Huykman

ENGINE MODIFICATIONS
Rebuilt by Tom Reiser, finned Pan covers, accessory horn, accessory oil gauge, accessory oil filter, mucho chrome

TRANSMISSION MODIFICATIONS
Chromed covers and kicker, chromed tank shifter, laminated shifter ball

FINISH
Painted by owner, Champion Yellow, black basecoat, clearcoat, original colors

FRAME MODIFICATIONS
1956 straightleg rigid, straightened

FRONT END MODIFICATIONS
Stock Hydra Glide with polished lower legs

FEATURED
Easyriders, December 1996

RADICAL CUSTOMS

Extreme Creativity on Two Wheels

Three o'clock in the morning, a tractor trailer rolls steadily across an interstate at 75 mph. The driver is alone except for a small caravan of Winnebagos a mile ahead on the dark desert highway. To each side is dense blackness and stillness, except for the occasional varmint with a death wish attempting one last freeway crossing. Then out of nowhere a sound interrupts the driver's solace. At first it suggests another vibration has taken hold of his 80,000-pound rig. He checks his gauges as the rumble grows louder. He inspects his rear view mirrors and is alarmed by a single headlight beam blasting virtually out of nowhere and coming up so fast that he pulls to the right to let it pass.

Looking down from his high perch above the road, he sees a slim 21-inch wheel split the night. A single Halogen headlight beam flickers in the chromed spokes. The front end is almost 25 inches over stock, and the chrome legs reach out for the front wheel like the slender arms of a woman reaching for the light ahead. Long upswept exhaust pipes reach the top of the chromed sissybar and shout stinging warnings. Then a rider appears on a majestic chassis that seems to glow in the night. A Viking of a man, with a massive mane of hair and a full beard, emerges and is gone in the twist of a throttle.

A chromed locomotive locked into its own track, the chopper follows the white line like a coke addict. As quickly as it arose, it was gone in a flash of chrome and metalflake. The radical chopper, more terrifying than a serpent in your bed, more startling than the sound of a .45 caliber automatic being cocked, sexier than a big-busted woman in a g-string.

The radical chopper is unlimited creativity in motion. The key word is unlimited. Our first radical chop landed in the very first issue of Easyriders as our cover bike. It was a wildly stretched, bare bones Knucklehead with a chromed extended springer front end and '70s-era psychedelic paint scheme. "Radical," from the judges' rulebook, includes, but is not limited to, severely modified frames. Once a builder operates on his frame, then ne rest of the bike begins to ransform around it. Creature omforts are dismissed with a nasty augh, to be replaced with a brave, evil-may-care attitude.

All this rings of subjective amblings, and that's a correct nalysis. There are no rules here. The radical chopper is a tougher east to ride; it takes a braver pilot, ne who doesn't need fuel gauges, ootboards, turn signals, large apacity fuel cells, passenger pegs, or uffy, long-distance seats. In the '50s, adical meant high handlebars. In the 60s, it meant long front ends. In ne '70s; it meant extremely altered hassis. In the '80s, it meant too nany drugs, and in the '90s it means oo much money.

The '90s have afforded builders ne world over an unlimited source of ustom components. Today, a man an build anything his unleashed nind will allow him to ride. Radical hoppers are vast departures from the riginal configuration, but in no pecific direction—just hang on and et go of preconceived notions. These reations ride the wild razor's edge.

Note the attention to detail on the triple trees. The slots are even continued to the underside of the billet aluminum components. Someone expected this machine to be closely scrutinized.

The seat is interesting because by itself it has no style. It's flat, painfully uncomfortable, yet perfect. It's the chopper rider's creed: "Cool before comfort, at all cost."

SPERMINATOR

SPERMINATOR

A radical chopper is just that, a giant step outside the norm or a sweeping change from the original. In other words, it's about getting crazy. Brad and his team of fantasy fabricators, paint wizards, and his parts posse escaped a mental institution to complete this machine.

Unsuspecting Brad rolled his reliable 1993 Harley-Davidson Fat Boy into The Hot Rod Shop in Summerville, South Carolina, one bright and shining day, strolled confidently up to the counter, and said, "Say, guys, can I get a paint job?"

It appeared to be a regular, run-of-the-mill body and fender joint, equipped with a paint booth, a thick layer of bondo dust, and a large supply of wet-and-dry sandpaper. But as each employee turned to look at the greenhorn customer, his confidence faded faster than the head on a flat beer. Will Limehouse, a man who, by all accounts, resembled a cross between Greg Allman and Jesus, stood up from behind a carefully restored 1940 Ford front fender and silently studied the bike with the finesse of a wine connoisseur tasting a vintage port. He looked at Brad only once, and in that electric instant Brad felt a pull that left him weak, as if his soul had been caged. Suddenly, other men appeared at the large industrial doorways.

MOTORCYCLE

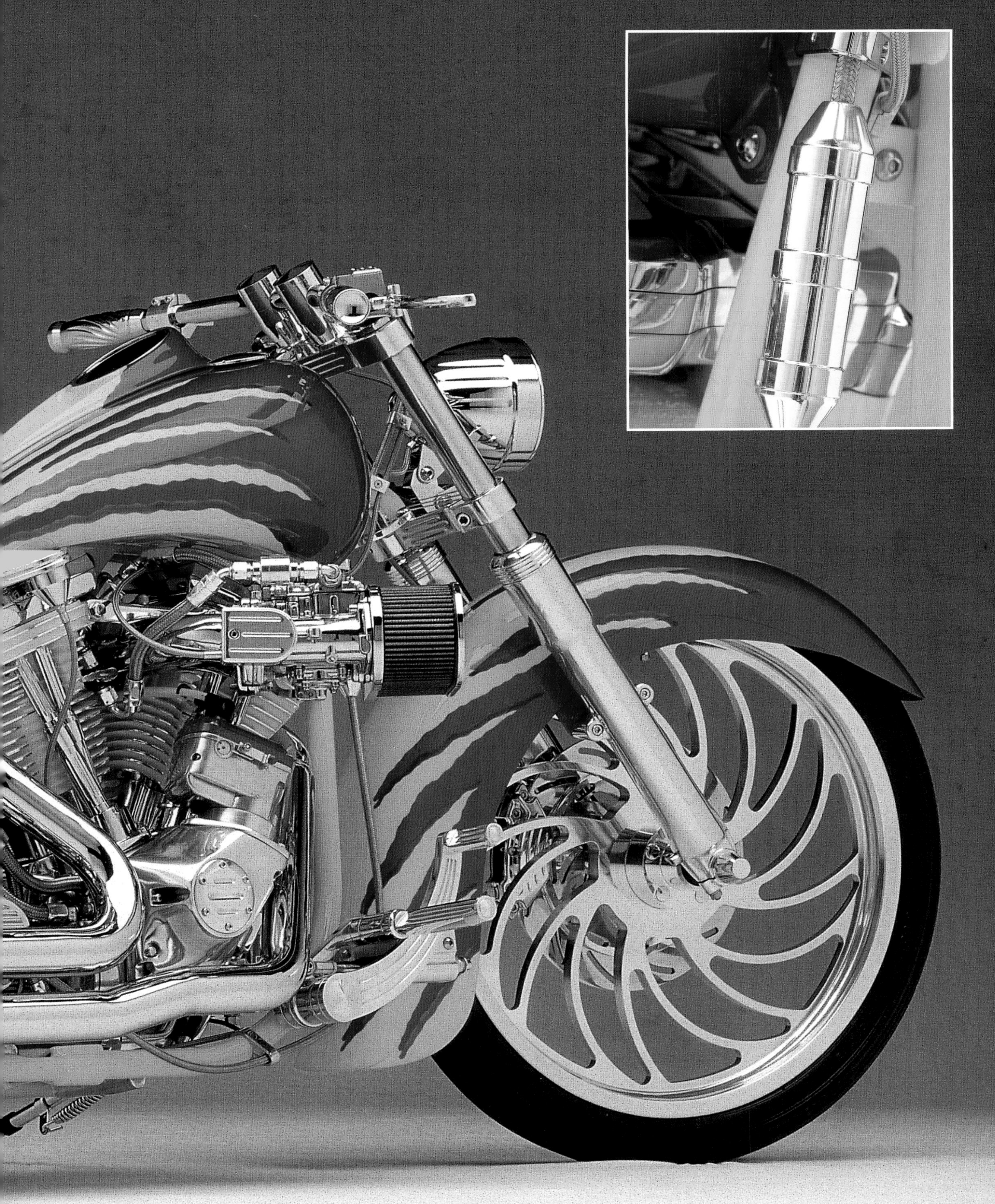

Johnny Hill from Tigger's Towing, a man so massive and strong he can bench press his own tow truck, came forward and whispered in Will's ear while gazing at Brad's bike. Out of nowhere, machinist David Seprish appeared and huddled with Will and Mr. Hill. Joey Venesky, a local upholsterer, stood in the door. A tall silhouette against the sunny backdrop, he carried a unique seat in his hands and held it out as if an offering to the custom gods.

The other men stopped their quiet chatter and looked at the seat. Then, without a word, they all nodded in unison. Immediately, wrenches began turning, air-sockets buzzed, lists were made, and as big Mr. Hill escorted Brad to the door, his bike was dismantled, the parts labeled and sorted.

Will made the fenders, David and Bobo's Speed & Custom took the engine, and Vinnie Minichiello, another member of the mysterious team, lit a torch, stretched the gas tank, and altered the frame. Ricky Machosek studied the seat for the perfect paint match and began concocting the mix of delicate hues. Hours turned into days, days into weeks, and weeks into months. Brad eventually returned to the shop insisting, "But I only wanted a paint job ... "

He was summarily asked to leave. More time spun past and he quietly and humbly returned, slinking into the shop to view the progress. Suddenly he discovered a wrench in one hand and a dripping sheet of 240-grit wet-and-dry in the other. He found himself working without a word as if guided by some spiritual goal. He could feel and sense the flow of the fenders and the polished surfaces of the engine as Johnny completed the rebuild.

Soon all he needed to hear was the phone ring and an ominous voice on the other end saying, "Get to the cave." Brad would immediately haul his ass to the shop and work tirelessly, sensing completion was near.

Ricky completed the paint and a clean cloth was laid beside a bench displaying the painted and polished engine and trans. Then, as if a signal flare had been shot into the sky, final assembly began. Voilà ... nothing to it.

SPERMINATOR

The exhaust pipes are carefully slashed at just the right length to allow the fender to be the final touch to the overall look of the bike The fender is carefully mounted to a radically modified swingarm, again, to purposely see that the it is left untouched.

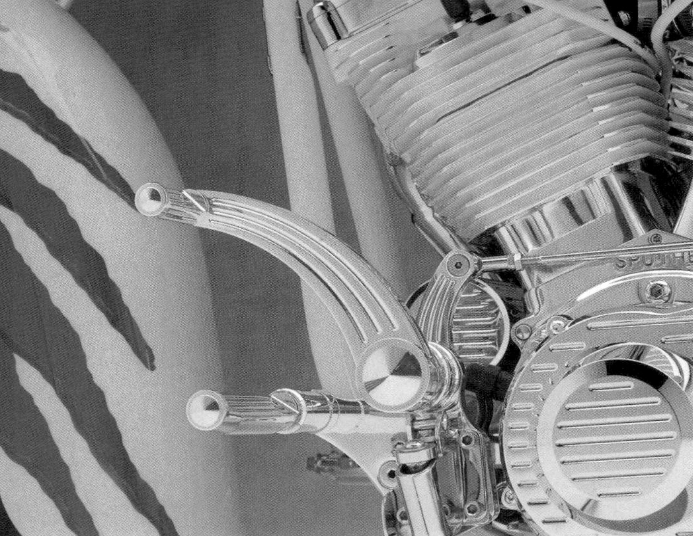

Another example of detailing is the shifting mechanism. Most builders who choose slots as a theme use whatever is available. This team made absolutely sure that every component matched perfectly.

he lines of this machine are its greatest sset. The overall design flows with perfect ymmetry, and the paint and detailing spare o expense to enhance the gilded rule.

YEAR AND MAKE
1993 Harley-Davidson

OWNER
Brad Castleberry

MODEL
Fat Boy

BUILDER
The Hot Rod Shop, Brad, Will, Vinnie, Joey, Ricky, and Johnny

ENGINE MODIFICATIONS
96-inch stroker, S&S lower end, Sputhe cases, Dave Mackie heads, S&S pistons, Sifton cam, Dell 'Orto carburetor, Pro-One exhaust

TRANSMISSION MODIFICATIONS
Backcut gears

FINISH
Molding by Vinnie Minichiello, painted by Rick Machosek, yellow, violet PPG paint

FRAME MODIFICATIONS
Raked, stretched, shaved, swingarm cut in half

FRONT END MODIFICATIONS
Accutronix forks, shortened 2 inches

FEATURED
Easyriders, October 1996

FANTASY

This bike flows like the wind. Its classic lines take onlookers on a journey in creamy pearlescent white paint, along careful contoured sheet metal, and into a cloud-like wind, like a billowing sail in the gulf of Mexico.

FROM FLORIDA

The radical custom takes on many forms and this pearl white, high-powered whisper of a cloud demonstrates the difference between radical and chopper. Choppers have tough, historical styling—stripped bikes with long front ends and high bars. They were the beginning of the custom trend. This scooter, built by Savage Cycle Works in Pompano

With the advent of LED lighting systems, a builder can cut slots in the rear fender and place strips of the highly reliable, extremely bright material in place behind the fender.

Beach, Florida, reeks more of a '30s automobile than a chopped Harley from the '50s. Hey, that's the beauty of custom bikes. Directions and styles are unlimited ... well, almost.

In this case, the emphasis was on the cosmetic appearance of the bike. There are no modifications to the transmission, and the engine mods are limited, but Lonnie Cantrell and his crew spent more than 500 hours building a "work of art that really works," as Lonnie puts it. The machining and fabrication were destined to become intricate and complicated, but the project moved steadily, if slowly, forward. Distinctive side panels were hand-formed from sheet metal, concealing the bike's battery and electronics, and a pair of maxi-blast air horns worthy of a Mack truck were installed beneath them. To maintain the scooter's trim profile, Lonnie changed out the bike's original front end in favor of a mid-glide setup and a narrow wheel. This effect was further enhanced by manufacturing new triple trees and refabricating the lower legs to blend with the new rear shock tubes.

Creating the one-piece handlebars required first removing 3½ inches of metal, then welding on the risers from a set of Ness bars. All the wiring is hidden by specially fabricated panels, front and back. The taillights utilize small but bright LEDs within the three chevrons on either side of the rear fender.

And by the way, four Dyna Wide Glide fenders were sacrificed to fabricate the two complimenting this bike. Final details included the fan-shaped custom dash, the louvers in the side panels, the shock tubes and exhaust pipes, not to mention the exotic, Ostrich inlaid seat.

There you have it, the broad strokes of a custom motorcycle. You'd be surprised how incomplete the big changes are without the fine details. Look closely and you'll see that virtually everything metal remaining on the bike is chrome, or polished. Look at the cable guides on the clutch cable, the axle caps, and the finely machined side mount license plate bracket. The bike's owner, Doctor Don Tanner, chose matching Arlen Ness footboards, controls, and engine accents to complete the accessories list.

Finally, assembly takes all the components and either creates a wonderful masterpiece or turns the whole mismatched mess into a bar brawl. This scooter was completed with the same level of care and talent as was injected into the construction of all the separate elements. Everything fits to a "T," and is finished properly. Don should be proud.

The drive train of this motorcycle is modified only slightly. The real alterations in overall appearance are accomplished through the hand-formed panels, fenders, tank, and headlight housing.

Another recent fad, not new but frequently seen, is the matching seat-to-paint scheme. More variety of dyes and improved manufacturing processes equals more seats built to match paint.

YEAR AND MAKE
1995 Harley-Davidson

OWNER
Don Tanner

MODEL
Dyna Wide Glide

BUILDER
Lonnie Cantrell, Savage Cycle Works

ENGINE MODIFICATIONS
Sachs Racing Engines heads, S&S carburetor, Crane cam, Savage Cycle Works exhaust

TRANSMISSION MODIFICATIONS
None

FINISH
Molding and paint by Savage Cycle Works, silver, white pearl urethane by House of Kolor

FRAME MODIFICATIONS
Dyna Wide Glide chassis, raked 41 degrees

FRONT END MODIFICATIONS
Dyna forks, modified lower legs, wide trees switched to mid glide

FEATURED
Easyriders, December 1996

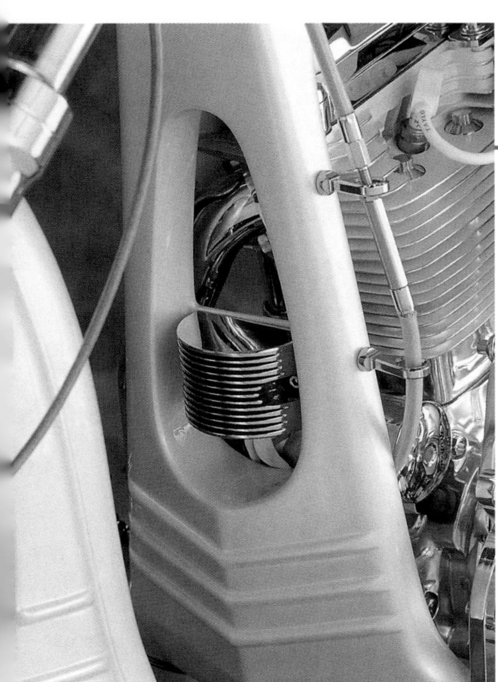

Air dams became popular with a well-known group of builders, the Hamsters, in the '80s. In some cases they hide electrical or unsightly oil coolers or filters; in this case, it frames the voltage regulator.

THE MASTERPIECE

This surfer-turned-bike builder is one of the newest young talents in the industry. Check the overall style of this motorcycle. His eye for flow and proportion is matched by his quality workmanship.

And now for a sordid story about the growth of a builder. Mike Maldonado grew up on the sunny, rock 'n' roll streets of San Juan Capistrano in Southern California. As a kid he spent little time in school and lots of time with his knees on a surfboard. He learned little of art, history, or the social sciences.

His mission was simple: maintain a fine tan, keep his hair well below shoulder length, and find and capture as many beach babes as possible. For years he perfected his pick-up lines and bikini-unraveling

From the rear, the bike has as much style as from the front. There are no extra panels that don't belong; it's just enough without going overboard.

style. He learned how to live handsomely on five bucks a week, how to change clothes on the beach without being detected, and how to maintain his sport and his vehicle—his surfboard.

He had no need to work; his folks were successful and rarely around. Besides, working interrupts early morning swells, the best tanning hours of the day, and making love in the afternoon. Mike was well on his way to a life as a beach bum. But there came a time when friends his age drifted off to become drug addicts, punk rockers, lawyers, and full-time felons. Confused as to which direction was appropriate, he went surfing off the coast of Cardiff and meditated to the gods of the sparkling sand, the prince of checkered bikinis, and the devil in the deep blue sea. While he floated aimlessly, sharks circling beneath his dangling legs, his bobbing surfboard bumped another. The board belonged to Jim Waggaman, a Hamster (a world-renowned group of bike builders) and bike builder. They spoke briefly in Surfonics, but Mike noted a sense of something more devious in Jim's eyes and followed him up the dunes to Jim's old diesel truck stop, where Mike discovered a den of custom motorcycles. Soon Mike was working on bikes with the same passion usually reserved for a gnarly wave.

One morning, not long after this experience, Mike woke up in his room, his late morning nap interrupted by his loving mother piling his red wagon with 200 surfing posters, several boxes of Surfing and Easyriders magazines and 400 ratty T-shirts. He was moving out. It was a day of reckoning and time for him to make a life-altering choice.

He could don his surf baggies and return to the sand, go to law school, take drugs, or slip into the motorcycle jacket hanging on the hook. The quandary was immense. He studied his feet and the adjacent beach sandals or his ratty biker boots. Just then his alarm went off and "Born to be Wild" by Steppenwolf filled the room. His decision was made—no more surfing, drugs, or thoughts of suing half the world. His mission was clear: He would become a bike bum and someday have his custom work published in Easyriders.

Shortly afterward Mike met Larissa and John Daley of San Diego, California. Impressed with his initial two-wheeled creations, they turned a 1995 FXR over to Mike and gave him free creative reign.
With his surfboard repair skills and an eye for girls' bodies, he went to work. "I wanted the bike to appear as a single, flowing piece," Mike said. He succeeded. With each new bike project, his prowess grows like a perfect wave.

The engine is nestled within a flowing frame, air dam, stretched tank, oil reservoir, and panel beneath it to hide the electric starter. Only the most complimentary components remain visible.

YEAR AND MAKE
1996 Harley-Davidson

OWNER
Larissa and John Daley

MODEL
FXR California Special

BUILDER
Mike Maldonado

ENGINE MODIFICATIONS
Carl's Speed Shop 98-inch stroker, S&S lower end, S&S cases, S&S pistons, Carl's Speed Shop heads, Carl's cam, S&S carburetor, Stankov exhaust, JIMS lifters

TRANSMISSION MODIFICATIONS
Belt Drives Limited (BDL) Belt Drive, RC Components wheel sprocket

FINISH
Molding by Mike Maldonado and J. More, paint by Maldonado, brandy mix House Of Kolor paint

FRAME MODIFICATIONS
Modified by Maldonado and Stankov, 39-degree rake, 3-inch stretch, welded in rear fender

FRONT END MODIFICATIONS
Maldonado modified cowling, painted and polished

FEATURED
Easyriders, September 1996

Look at how the artist has massaged the frame to grace the fender and capture the shock absorber along the way without interrupting the lines. The taillights are sculpted into the swingarm, and the rear fender fits the tire perfectly.

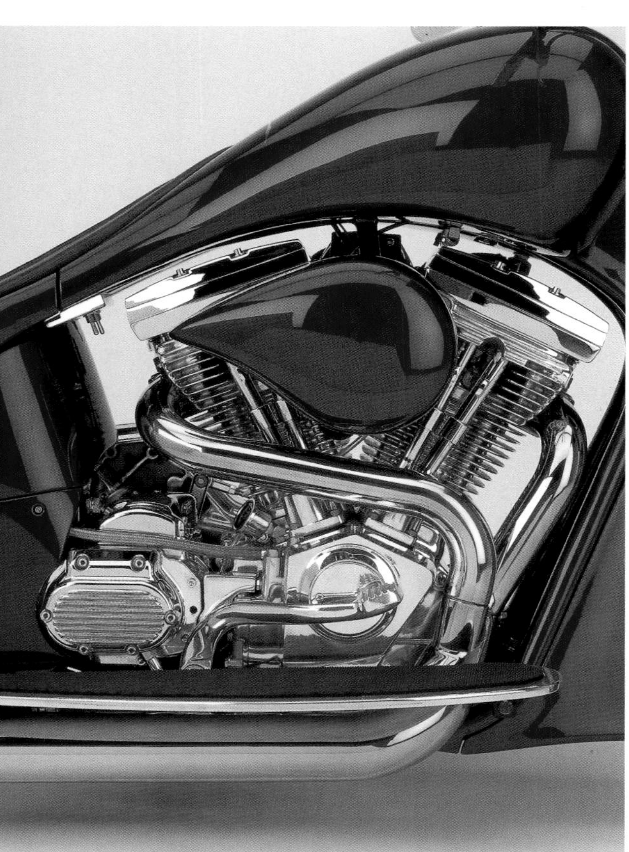

CANAILLE ROUGE

Clean lines, a tight chassis, and precision machining make this monster fly. Other than the stretched and hand-fabricated sheet metal, everything is billet aluminum.

To billet or not to billet? This bike represents the best in billet engineering ... well, sorta. I mean, the damn thing is billet from one end to the other. The process of manufacturing billet aluminum parts is simple and accurate, but costly.

Originally, billet represented the finest materials being used to enhance strength and finish. Obviously, if the finest quality material is being machined, and not melted or heat-distorted, it won't be porous, affording the finest chrome adhesion and smoothest surface for the polishing wheel.

That was the technology a couple of years ago. Today, the machining stations save every last chip, which is salvaged to return another day. In addition, new casting methods are setting new standards against the billet rule. Cast parts, which are much cheaper to manufacture, are coming back into vogue. They look as good—and are just as strong—as their billet counterparts.

When Jesse James set out to build this bike for Cajun Mike Guidry, while he was with Boyd's (he's since founded West Coast Choppers in Paramount, California), the goal was to create a red flash that was light, low, and compact. Jesse was the ideal creator, as his style revolves around those precepts. At the time he had just designed the billet swingarm. He coupled the tail section with Boyd's wheels, a billet pulley, billet triple

The only tin you'll find on this machine is on the pipes and headlight. It's all aluminum from that point on.

trees, gas cap, risers, accessories, mirrors, and Performance Machine billet brakes and controls, and the bike became a nasty 89-cubic-inch road rocket.

Light, tight, and ready to fight is the slogan behind this alligator-wrestling red marvel, and Mike Guidry was as pleased as any owner could be with the outcome.

YEAR AND MAKE
1993 Jesse James

OWNER
Mike Guidry

MODEL
Soft James

BUILDER
Jesse James

ENGINE MODIFICATIONS
89-cubic-inch S&S lower end, S&S pistons, Delkron cases, Patrick Racing billet heads, Lieneweber cam, Mikuni 42mm carburetor, Jesse James/Hot Rods By Boyd (HRBB) exhaust

TRANSMISSION MODIFICATIONS
Polished case, mid-mount shifting, Boyd's sprocket

FINISH
Painted by HRBB and Keith Russell, red Dupont paint

FRAME MODIFICATIONS
Chassis by Jesse James and HRBB, Outlaw swingarm

FRONT END MODIFICATIONS
Mid glide, shortened 2 inches

FEATURED
Easyriders, April 1996

JOURNEY IN FLIGHT

This bike contains top-of-the line billet accessories from Arlen Ness and Performance Machine. What wasn't sourced was machined in-house, such as the air cleaner and the matching dual coil cover on the opposite side.

This is another sharp example of a Pro Street bike with a heavier look. Larger fenders, a stretched dresser tank, and the heavy-looking air dam coupled with the deep, dark blue paint give it an ominous air. The owner, Michael Shiff, raises championship horses and rode motorcycles as a kid, but, once you're bitten, the bug never crawls far from the hearth. No matter how many horses he owned and raced over the years, that addiction for the wind in his hair and the need for two-wheeled speed never diminished.

A few years ago the addiction struck hard, and Michael was forced to abolish the motorcycle 12-step program. He jumped back into the asphalt tangle with a new Softail and high-tailed it to Colorado. But on the return trip, inspiration struck and he resolved to cement his love for riding motorcycles and horses into an appropriate tribute.

First he researched equine art books for the proper images. Once he found what he was looking for, he flew to Texas to meet with the creator at Bonny Fine Art of Dallas. She blessed his concept, and he connected with Lonnie Cantrell of Savage Cycle Works in Pompano Beach, Florida, to launch the project. Lonnie is a master when it comes to bringing two-wheeled dreams to reality. In the case of this fast flight of fantasy, the dream was realized with class and style to create a steel stallion for the 21st century.

JOURNEY IN FLIGHT

This machine couples dark purple panels with a matching leather seat and tough-looking billet accessories.

The appearance of the automotive spoiler on his Savage Cycle Works, Kenny Boyce custom llowed the builder to conceal the taillight. The turn signals disappear in the fender rails.

YEAR AND MAKE
1994 Harley-Davidson

OWNER
Michael Shiff

MODEL
Pro Street

BUILDER
Savage Cycle Works

ENGINE MODIFICATIONS
98.5-cubic-inch S&S lower end, S&S pistons, Delkron cases, STD heads, Dyna single fire ignition, S&S Super G carburetor, Bub Stepmother exhaust

TRANSMISSION MODIFICATIONS
Shaved and polished case

FINISH
Molding and paint by Hyena Graphics, blurple House of Kolor paint, Bonny Fine Art design

FRAME MODIFICATIONS
Kenny Boyce Pro Street Chassis, 33.5-degree rake

FRONT END MODIFICATIONS
SJP forks from Holland, Arlen Ness triple trees, custom fender

FEATURED
Easyriders, July 1995

PURPLE DAZE

The front end appears European with the performance White Power forks, the trimmed traditional cowling, and elongated and painted fork covers.

Now here's a confusing set of circumstances. A couple of us had mechanical problems on our way to Sturgis, South Dakota. We pulled into a small, recently renovated Harley-Davidson dealership in Wyoming. Nice place, but the owner and main wrench in the back didn't have much respect for us or our motorcycles. "I don't like working on this custom shit," he said in a surly tone. We glared in unison and he worked on 'em anyway. Traditionally, dealers and the factory scorned the chopper rider. In the case of this bike, the opposite is true.

Russ Tom and his dad, Carmen, own Downtown Harley-Davidson in Seattle, Washington, and they love custom motorcycles. Even before the younger Tom got involved, Carmen was building bad-ass bikes. This ride is a perfect example of what they're capable of—high-tech Arlen Ness accessories, Pro-One billet wheels, and top-of-the-line Performance Machine billet, 6-piston caliper brakes. Russ machined a left-side manifold and his sheetmetal people stretched the gas tanks and made the fenders and panels. Then they lowered it by shortening the front end 2 inches and the rear 2 1/5 by installing high-tech Fornelli shocks.

This scooter depicts state-of-the-art custom work, direct from a hometown dealership. But do me a favor, don't tell anyone at the factory—they frown on such behavior.

PURPLE DAZE

Downtown Harley-Davidson in Seattle, Washington, is noted for its ability to detail engines and pack in custom performance.

Note the way the fender was designed to hide the top of the shock body and fastener, plus the fender rails and an obtrusive taillight.

YEAR AND MAKE
1990 Harley-Davidson

OWNER
Curtis Lang

MODEL
FXRS

BUILDER
Russ Tom/Downtown Harley-Davidson (DHD), Seattle, Washington

ENGINE MODIFICATIONS
80-cubic-inch Harley rebuilt by Mike Bradshaw at DHD, Dyna ignition Street heads, Andrews E47 cam, S&S leftside carburetor, DHD exhaust, manifold by DHD

TRANSMISSION MODIFICATIONS
None

FINISH
Molding and painting by Custom Classics, candy purple urethane, special paint by Custom Classics

FRAME MODIFICATIONS
Trimmed and molded by Custom Classics

FRONT END MODIFICATIONS
White Power upside-down front end, 2 inches under, custom FL-styled nacelle by DHD

FEATURED
Easyriders, March 1996

IT'S ALL TOO MUCH

Battistini's has a very close working relationship with Arlen Ness in the states. Therefore, their bikes are showcases of Arlen's accessories, and, wherever possible, they enhance the look with their own parts made to match.

This bike demonstrates why professional bike builders and contractors stay alive from one project to another, as opposed to the lone builder who abandons his family and friends, giving up riding for months to finish his dream machine in the solace of his garage (because his entire family left him), only to go slowly mad. The professional spreads the stress. That's the case with this Battistinis-built Showstar.

Battistinis is located in Bournemouth, England, where the project began under the guidance of Arlen Ness, clear across the ocean in San Leandro, California. That's spreading the frustration!

The engine was built by the masters of performance at Carl's Speed Shop in Daytona, Florida. Carl pumped the Sportster to 98 cubes, puffing out 115 brake horsepower. While in England, Jeff Duval and his crew wove the exhaust through the frame subassemblies and three hand-hammered steel bodywork panels. And to prevent it from frying the paint, the panels were protected with automotive asbestos and gold reflectors.

Kirk Jennings spent 88 hours prepping the sizable job while the painter paced the shop floor and tapped his watch. American painter extraordinaire Jeff McCann was called in to provide the bike's colorful mantle. Jeff took one look at the job and went back to port to find the next ship out. Like a sailor from a bygone era, he was mugged and dragged back to the shop and pressed into service. As you can tell, he's the man. And the Battistinis team survived another project, to begin the next.

IT'S ALL TOO MUCH

YEAR AND MAKE
1995 Harley-Davidson

OWNER
Carl Wilson

MODEL
Showstar

BUILDER
Battistinis Custom Cycles

ENGINE MODIFICATIONS
1600cc Sportster Engine by Carl Morrow, Crane single-fire Hi-4 ignition, Axtell pistons, Carl's heads and cam, stainless steel custom exhaust, S&S Super G carburetor

TRANSMISSION MODIFICATIONS
4-speed gearbox, Barnett clutch

FINISH
Molding by Kirk Jennings, paint by Jeff McCann, virgin white and yellow Deltron urethane, graphics by Jeff McCann

FRAME MODIFICATIONS
John Parry-built frame with Jeff Duval's specs, 38-degree rake, 6-inch stretch

FRONT END MODIFICATIONS
39mm mid glide, extended 2 inches, chromed FXR legs, Ness narrow glide kit

FEATURED
Easyriders, February 1996

This extensively modified Sportster still retains a sporty appearance due to the styling to the frame, tank, and fenders, the exhaust system, the light, narrow front end, and the Performance Machine wheels.

Note the carefully designed billet taillight hidden under the fender. It works effectively but does not disturb the profile of the motorcycle.

AN UGLY IDEA

Ah, the smell of a Panhead (1948-1965), the look of the tin rocker covers, and the sound of Harley-Davidson history. Many motorcycle maniacs began their two-wheeled obsession with a motorcycling experience that occurred during early, formative years. In other words, when we were kids our parents beat us into shape. Spotting motorcycles was like a prisoner finding a chrome file in his soup.

Cliff Grayson had such an experience at the tender age of 13. His father, a mechanic, had helped push a friend's broken-down bike into his garage. When the two left to get parts, Cliff crept into the stall, filed the points, and gave the bike a kick. The scoot sprang to life.

Later, the two adults returned to find the bike gone. Much later, Cliff returned to find the two men waiting: one pensive, the other furious. The ass-whipping stayed with him for years, but the ride stayed longer.

Some years and many bikes later, Cliff began to build his ultimate custom. His talent with tools and his love of motorcycles is apparent in every aspect of this bike. It's the love of a bike's lines, the feeling of accomplishment when a custom masterpiece is finally completed, and a passion for freedom, all rolled into one. Every nut and bolt on this FL breathes liberty into the man who caressed its curves in order to bring it to life. For once born, a Harley's life is dedicated to making confined men free.

This custom formula combines the old (a 1954 power train), with the new (billet wheels from Sturgis and the latest in braking technology from Performance Machine). Upsweep pipes are old school, but not the billet clamps that hold them securely in place.

YEAR AND MAKE
1954 Harley-Davidson

OWNER
Cliff Grayson

MODEL
FL

BUILDER
Eyeball Engineering

ENGINE MODIFICATIONS
Magneto ignition, Sifton cam, Dell 'Orto carburetor, Paughco and E.E. exhaust, Pro-One air cleaner, Sifton lifters, billet cam cover

TRANSMISSION MODIFICATIONS
Backcut gears

FINISH
Molding and paint by Greg Pettigrew, black lacquer, graphics by Greg

FRAME MODIFICATIONS
Paughco rigid chassis, 34-degree rake, 2-inch stretch

FRONT END MODIFICATIONS
All-chrome wide glide, hidden bolts on trees

FEATURED
Easyriders, August 1996

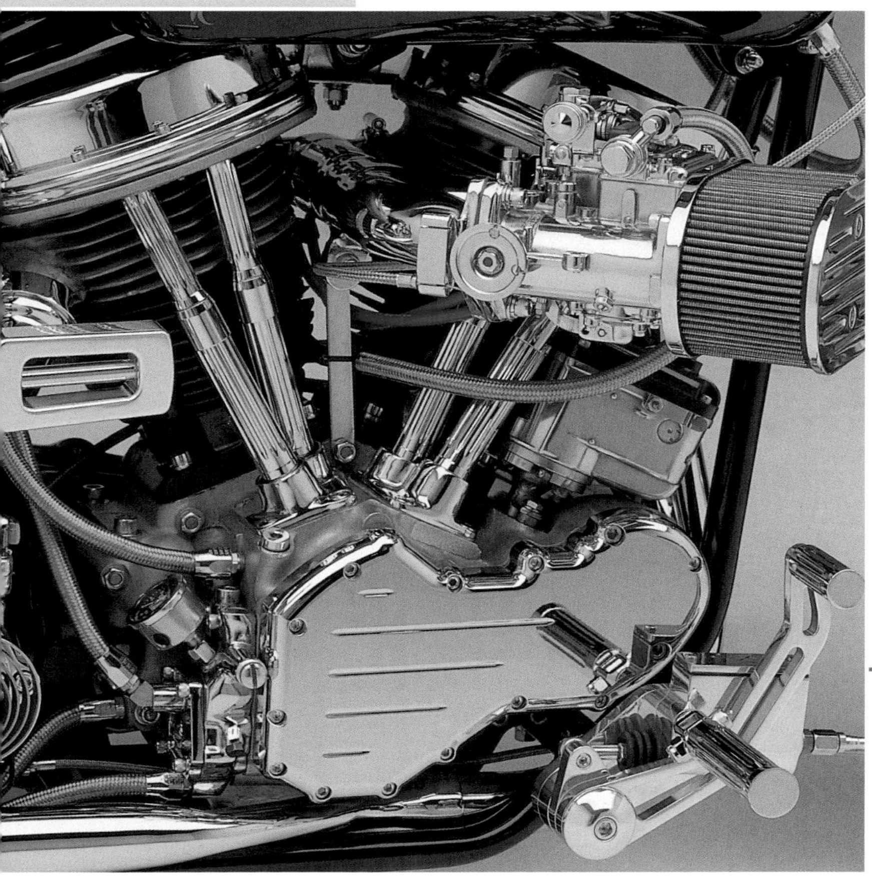

The engine may be from the '50s, but its magneto ignition, Dell 'Orto carburetor, Sifton cam, and billet aluminum cam cover bring it into the here and now.

SWEET INSPIRATION

For a different look, the owner coupled a billet aluminum rear wheel and Iron Pegasus brakes with a twisted-spoke wire front, but he matched the RC Components stainless steel rotors.

In today's world of talented metal workers and sky-high technology, anything's possible. So much so, that a hot rod builder like Wink Eller can hit his head against the bed stand one night and, in a daze, glance at an antique car magazine, spy a $370,000 Bugatti EB110—featuring a 553hp, V12 engine, double-overhead cams, 60 valves, and four turbochargers—and say, "Sure, I can build something like that."

When that car was built in the '40s, the body was constructed from Nomex honeycomb, sandwiched by carbon fiber-reinforced plastic beneath an aluminum skin. Wink woke up and went to work with sheet-metal fabricator Simon, of Wink's Custom Cycles in Santa Ana, California. His shop's emphasis is on performance, so this bike flies as well as it looks.

"I rode it to Laughlin, Nevada, and I plan to ride it to Sturgis," Wink says. All right, I have a confession. I'm also working with several builders to perform a big, swooping miracle. It weights three tons, and needs an extra engine to get it down the street. That's the difference between a man who knows, and a man who dreams.

SWEET INSPIRATION

The hand-formed tank takes on a dual role. It houses the fuel through a billet aluminum flush mounted tank cap and the speedometer.

YEAR AND MAKE
1995 Harley-Davidson

OWNER
Wink Eller

MODEL
Winkster

BUILDER
Wink Eller

ENGINE MODIFICATIONS
Wink-built 80-cubic-inch engine, Crane ignition, Branch JE pistons, House of Horsepower cases, Branch/Wink's heads, Wink's MS-17 cam, S&S carburetor, Wink's exhaust

TRANSMISSION MODIFICATIONS
Andrews gears, BDL belt drive

FINISH
No molding, Butch Brinza paint, candy brandy and grape House of Kolor materials

FRAME MODIFICATIONS
Chassis built by Arlen Ness, Wink, and Simon, rubbermount 37-degree frame with hidden wiring

FRONT END MODIFICATIONS
39mm FXR forks, polished trees

FEATURED
Easyriders, September 1995

GOTCHA

Long, low, trimmed Softail with every detail and billet enhancement known to man including wheels rotors and pulley. This was on man's odyssey and hewas successful right down to the polished stainless steel Allen bolts.

So many motorcycles are built from dreams—visions formed in cold garages late at night. A man doesn't build a motorcycle in the same way he fixes a refrigerator. Each chromed and pearlescent painted element of this machine was painstakingly thought through after a full day's work. Don Grassie often lingered in his garage into the wee hours of the morning, losing entire weekends while his wife roamed the lonely halls of their Myrtle Beach home in South Carolina, worrying and wondering whether he would ever appear again and resume his responsibilities as a husband.

Too often garages become Dr. Jekyll's laboratory. What emerges after several nights of pondering the depth of chrome is a new man, one who is possessed by the finish of polished aluminum, nicked by errant wrenches and demented by the smell of fresh paint. He's a man frustrated from the day he purchases his first component until the day he can shift into fifth and feel all 96 inches propel him onto the open roads and beyond.

Few marriages endure the extreme rigors of a bike building project. Few women know the costly cure for a

This front end is a catalog display of everything high-tech available to the Harley market today.

man waiting to ride, his fingernails worn and frayed, his life seemingly on the brink of collapse. Hell, woman, buy him another bike before he goes out of his mind. He can sell it when his dream machine is complete, but the man must ride ... or perish.

YEAR AND MAKE
1996 Harley-Davidson

OWNER
Don Grassie

MODEL
FXSTC

BUILDER
B&M Cycles/Richard Martin

ENGINE MODIFICATIONS
96-inch S&S engine kit, RevTech ignition, Drag Specialties exhaust

TRANSMISSION MODIFICATIONS
None

FINISH
Molding by Ronnie Wright, House Of Kolor pearl white/magenta paint, tank graphics

FRAME MODIFICATIONS
Pro-One Pro Fat Chassis, 38-degree rake, 5-inch stretch

FRONT END MODIFICATIONS
Wide glide with Pro-One triple trees

FEATURED
VQ magazine, February 1997

HOT PERFORMERS

MOLDING STYLE WITH BRUTE SPEED

Sure, this chapter represents the best in performance customs from the pages of *Easyriders* magazine. But there's something more to the subject than that, something that has the same irreverent power as a fighter plane buzzing an enemy aircraft carrier. That's the point of chops, bobs, or custom bikes. They're as illegal as a joyride on a hot summer day. Now, take these elements and pour them into a blender: two parts illegal, two parts chrome, two parts urethane metalflake, and two parts raw power. Now stir that sucker on high, and you have the aphrodisiac of the gods, a high so consuming, so addictive, that few who enter the saloon ever leave the same. I can't imagine a higher high. There's nothing more intriguing, aggressive, or sensual than the look, feel, and full-throttle action of a high-performance bike.

It wasn't always as easy to attain that gut-gripping speed as it is in the high-tech '90s. Before the '60s, experimentation was the order of the day. Riders cut the mufflers off their bikes and tried new carburetors. Then when the Shovelhead arrived on the scene, some of the freaks on the block, including myself, dug through parts bins in search of UL wheels to install in the crankcases of the late-model bikes. That simple modification took a tame 74-cubic-inch Big Twin to the heights of the massive 80-inch motor. The 80-inch configuration is standard today; in fact, it's the bottom of the performance food chain.

Then came the '80s, and the Evolution engine was followed closely by performance-minded engineers who were ready to take the much-hailed Evo to the work bench for alterations. They weren't blowing smoke, either. S&S Cycle in Viola, Wisconsin, developed stroked wheels in proportions ranging from 87- to 103-inch motors. Carburetors sprung from talented minds. Exhaust systems, ignition systems, brakes, blowers, fuel injection systems, turbos, and nitrous all took a turn for the high-tech Harley application. Computers allowed the manufacturers to investigate every component with simulated tests. Quality coupled with a vast network of information took 60 horse stock Big Twins to 100 horses and beyond.

In this case, I'll mention the Japanese sport bikes, probably the highest tech bikes ever built, with power bands that could easily snap a mortal's neck, and speeds exceeding 160 mph. A standard modified Harley can't compete with that technology, but there's more to a ride on a Harley than simply speed. There's that illegal nature, that ability to stand out from the masses, passing them as if they're anchored to the asphalt, dodging the tin cages as if wielding bullwhips in a crowd of cows. The point is power coupled with high, irreverent style. That's the way it is, and we like it.

So, now the '90s emerged onto the scene as the Harley market peaked, and every performance-minded talent in the industry and out-of-work aerospace engineer devoted time and energy to making the custom bikes fly. Even some automotive giants began to look hard at the Harley emporium. Edelbrock entered the market with the QwikSilver carburetor; ACCELL, owned by Mr. Gasket, developed a line of electrical components for the Harley rider; and automotive cam manufacturers, such as Crane, developed highly successful lines of performance cams.

In the early days, performance often signified scoots that were stripped down to dispense with the added weight. Now, all the technology in the world is available, plus the components to make any Harley fly farther and faster, no matter how heavy.

So take a fast ride on the wild side and check out the bikes that not only look good, but are guaranteed to turn your knuckles white in the time it takes to twist a grip.

STREET DRAGON

The bike is low at the rear, as it should be, then tapers up and forward for a tough, dug-in appearance, as if it's ready to lunge at any time.

Reggie pointed out to us that Americans have it way too easy when it comes to customizing bikes. With 800 numbers, next day UPS, Federal Express, fax machines, modems, and now the Internet, we can communicate orders for parts, design drawings, create detailed descriptions, and deliver maps and money through the wind, over the airways, and across the vast cyber-highway for speedy delivery. In many cases you can have your cherished part the very next day. In fact, we yanks are such an impatient bunch that we're severely disappointed if the part isn't in our hot little hands overnight.

Life is too short. No time to lose. Move and groove. That girl isn't gonna stand on the street corner waiting for you forever. Yeah, we like it like that. But when Reggie and his Beaujolais-guzzling bros from the shores of France decided to bite the bullet and build this fast freak, they

The bottles on the front would normally indicate a high-pressure NOS nitrous system. In reality, they are the oil supply canisters for the engine.

Although this bike is not ridden at the drag strip on a regular basis, it certainly gives the impression of being designed and built for the racetrack.

didn't have access to the plethora of convenient avenues to parts, services, and accessories we have in the 50 states. Shipping costs across the pond can also be costly, to the point of being prohibitive. Then there's that bit about language barriers, hindering detailed communications, and the nasty wait for a product no one knows will work or fit until it arrives.

So Reggie and his partners broke open an old Jammer handbook and a number of classic *Easyriders* magazines and went to work modifying parts themselves. Check out the oil tank, fuel cell, radical frame, and hydraulic clutch.

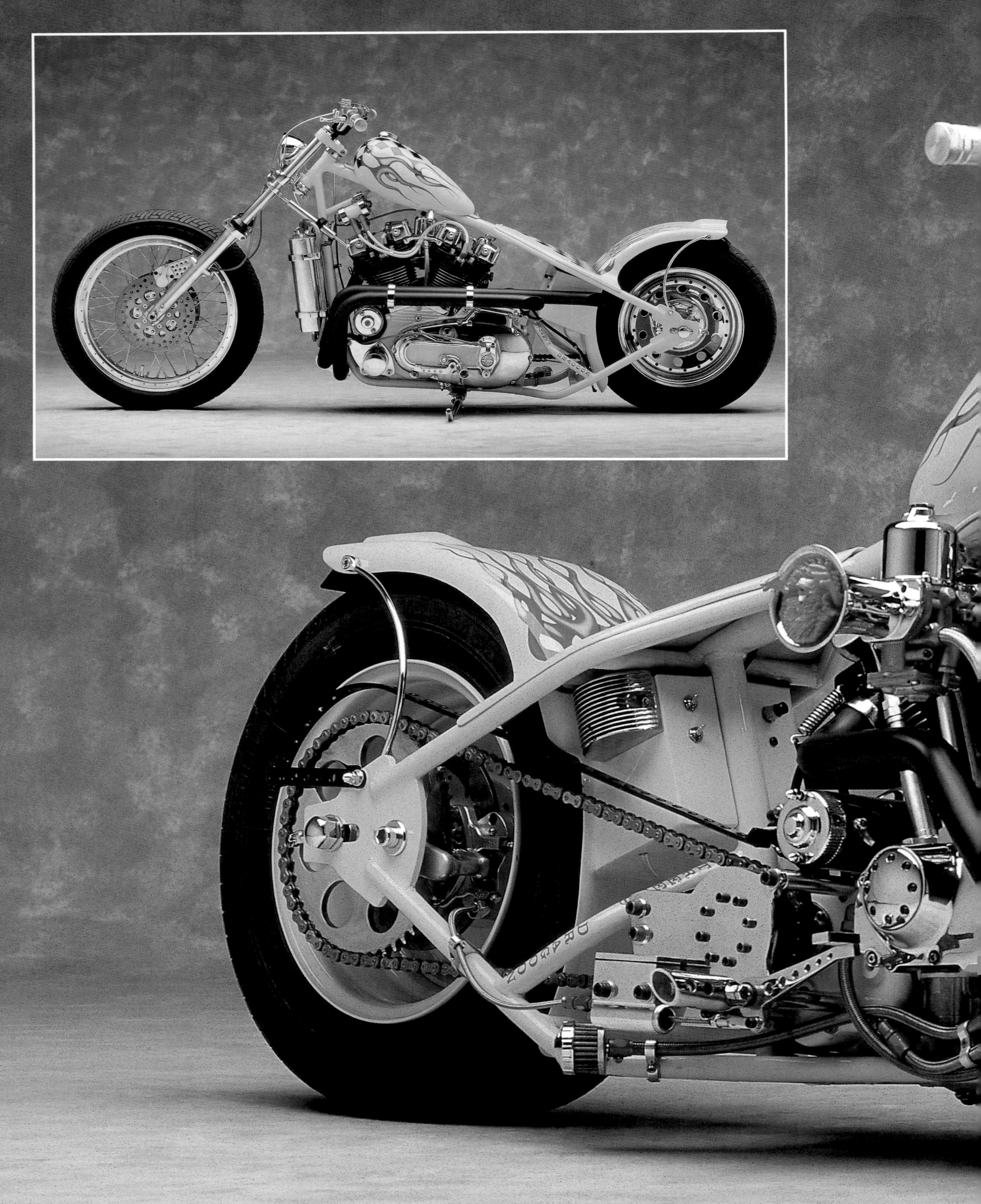
DRAGON

Reggie built confidence with every modification and each new component. Ultimately, his love of bikes caused Reg and his partner P.J. "Zan" Zanvit to open their own custom shop, Street Drag, and go into business for themselves. This low-slung, pipes-out-the-left-side, checkered and flamed street racer is their calling card all over Europe. With the assistance of Mino, Yankee, Wolf, "Le Prince", Pat d'Albi, Sophie, Coco Arthur, Enzo, Jules, and Giulia they've created a successful operation for fabricating lethal, leg-wettin' pavement-eaters.

Presently, as U.S. manufacturers such as Arlen Ness, Performance Machine, and major distributor Custom Chrome move outlets into Europe, Reggie and his band of chromed merry men will have access to many of the finest products in the world. It won't be a one-way trip, either. More European builders are creating parts these days that will ultimately land on U.S. shores and onto American bikes. The world is getting smaller, more efficient, and the girls get better looking all the time (I don't understand how that last bit got there, must be this French keyboard).

This is the epitome of a performance custom motorcycle. Check out the drag-strip-ready rear tire, the nitrous bottle-looking oil bags, the light frame, and the heavily modified engine. Weight was cut by drilling holes in everything, and the open velocity stack on the performance SU carburetor makes the scoot look like it's moving even when it's standing still. The checkered flag paint job has this bike poised for a race even when Reggie is nowhere near the machine.

Yes, this is what street performance customs are all about: an intimidating appearance coupled with ample power to back up the threat—and enough brakes to stop before the paddy wagon gets there.

STREET DRAGON

The engine is stripped and the tough street drag appearance comes from the exposed coils, bright spark plug wires, the handmade, black exhaust system and the large-mouth carburetor with velocity stack.

Note the no-pad seat and tiny taillight almost hidden by the license tags at the rear of the fender. The drilled chain guard and wheel completes the no-comfort, light look.

YEAR AND MAKE
Harley-Davidson

OWNER
Reggie Pottier

MODEL
XL

BUILDER
Street Drag

ENGINE MODIFICATIONS
1000cc S&S engine rebuilt by Street Drag, dual-point RevTech ignition, Wiseco pistons, modified dual-plug heads, Sifton Pro Stock cam, SU Rivera carburetor, Street Drag exhaust, Sifton lifters.

TRANSMISSION MODIFICATIONS
Andrews gears, billet by Zan, Street Drag Big W trans sprocket

FINISH
Painted by Michel, yellow lacquer, urethane, special paint by owner and Aclidé

FRAME MODIFICATIONS
Street Drag chassis by Street Drag, 39-degree rake, stretched, altered extensively

FRONT END MODIFICATIONS
Modified by Street Drag, chromed

FEATURED
Easyriders, April 1995

FOREVER WILD

A husband built this rolling work of art for his wife. Every element is hand-formed, like the handlebars, as if he were touching her gently as he massaged each part to life.

This motorcycle belongs to a woman who rides and lives in Paris, France. There's something ominous about the thought of a woman riding a bike of this caliber through the slippery, cobblestone streets of Paris, heading toward the dark and dank nightclub district on a machine reeking of dangerous curves and wild times.

Sure, her renowned European bike-building husband, Nicolas Chauvin, built this machine, but what difference would that make to a predatory onlooker? Nicolas started by moderately stretching and raking the fork neck. The frame was then modified to accommodate a rubbermounted oil tank, which was relocated under the seat and hidden from view by a molded-in, wraparound panel. The shapely air dam is made of sheet metal and molded to the bottom of the frame's tapering down-tubes. To top off the feminine lines of this feline motorcycle, the Sporty tanks were sliced into 25 pieces and radically reshaped.

When he completed the bodywork, Nicolas shot flashy, candy-metalflake maroon over a silver base to serve as a backdrop for his murals and graphics. Perhaps the sensual shape of the tank, the hip-like curvy rear fender and sloping breast air dam is a tribute to his wife's form.

This Parisian night crawler has sexiness written all over it. From the contoured tank to the hand-formed handlebars, this machine speaks femininity.

Check the twisted pipes, the exotic manifold, and the baby blue highlights on the engine, then try to imagine the sensual shape of the woman who rides it.

Maybe the vibrating button on the seat is meant to remind her to come home after a long night of riding. Hell, I don't know, but my hands are wringing with curiosity. I like my fantasy. Besides, this lady rider supervised every aspect of the project.

I've got to believe that while Nicolas is buried in bondo dust and grease, maintaining his distinguished reputation, Geraldine dresses for another Parisian night. While his welder hums in the garage, she slithers into the streets, dressed in painted-on leather pants, laced up the side of her shapely legs, and a tightly tailored vest. A pair of spiked black leather boots accents the ensemble. She pulls on a small set of fingerless gloves and a set of streak-like narrow sunglasses.

Her vest is bubbling over with sexiness as she waits for a man to skid around the corner of a 15-century chateau on an equally wild chopper, only to capture a glimpse of her lurid form disappearing into the night. He speeds to catch her. As she spies his single beam caressing the curves of her pink Sportster, the man is drawn to her lewd web of shapes and sounds. He races to meet her suggestive moves and check the carnal outfit she's wearing, revealing enough soft flesh to make any man's palms sweat. Suddenly she's a black widow drawing her masculine prey into her web. She teases him with a longing glance over her shoulder as he closes to her side just long enough to inhale her orgiastic scent. He opens his dry mouth to speak as she twists the throttle and the chase begins. They ride through the night, past monuments to the finest lovers and bravest men in French history, around neo-socialist high-rises, and

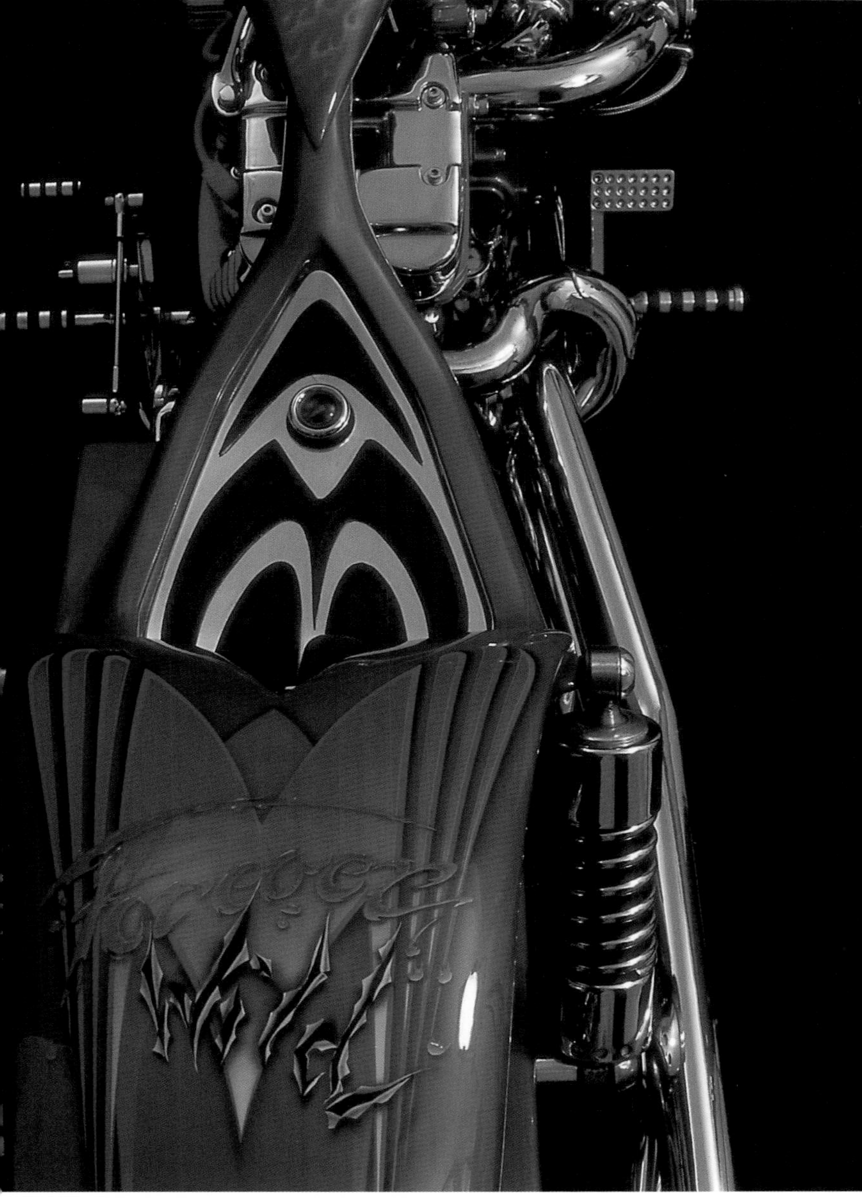

The seat is especially interesting with its hip-like fender and sensitive button. What could it mean?

YEAR AND MAKE
1995 Harley-Davidson

OWNER
Geraldine and Nicolas Chauvin

MODEL
Forever Wild Sportster

BUILDER
Nicolas Chauvin

ENGINE MODIFICATIONS
1200cc Harley motor, Dyna S Rivera ignition, Wiseco pistons, stainless steel Manley valves, Andrews V2 cam, homemade manifold, Dell 'Orto 40mm carburetor, exhaust by owner

TRANSMISSION MODIFICATIONS
Barnett Kevlar clutch, offset sprocket from Bartels' H-D

FINISH
Paint by Nicolas, magenta, blue, pink, red, yellow, candy metalflake, airbrushing by Nicolas

FRAME MODIFICATIONS
38-degree rake, 6-inch stretch, 11-inch Progressive Suspension shocks

FRONT END MODIFICATIONS
Inverted forks, 1-inch-over, polished, painted, GSXR with V-shaped triple trees

FEATURED
Easyriders, August 1996

between the most exclusive hotels on the West Bank. Passing the protective Gargoyles overlooking the gardens of Notre Dame, the glint in her eye narrows, her thighs warm and the button between her legs glows.

The game is over, and her prey is lost in the narrow streets, searching for the woman in black on the metallic pink Sportster. She returns home to the man who created the beast she rides.

AVON AND TODD

Light Brembo wheels and mono-shock suspension allow the Big Twin to handle the performance Avon tires through mountain curves as well as on the straight-aways.

Performance Harleys take on various shapes and styles, and, generally, this is not one of them. I mean, they usually look like radical choppers or drag bikes, not road racers. But when Tom Todd, the veteran bike builder and creative lead of G.T. Custom Cycles in Maryland, New York, received his commission from Avon Tires to build them a signature machine, he was the recipient of overwhelming inspiration.

Since the bike would represent one of the premier tire manufacturers in the world, and their line of tires encompasses everything from touring bikes and customs, to Japanese road racers, he decided to inject an international, intermodal, interesting flair into this build. "I wanted to

The Showa performance front end with fiberglass fender and Brembo brakes takes this heavy Harley into the realm of street racers.

construct a Harley that would corner as well as it went straight," Tom said, patting the seat of his mono-shock frame. "The mono-shock is the key."

In addition to the modifications it took to install the single rear shock to the swingarm and frame, the extremely light Brembo wheels, brakes and Showa front end finished the curve-hugging chassis.

A custom alloy swingarm lightens the rear of the frame. The Brembo brakes and carbon fiber Vance and Hines muffler work with the high-tech theme.

New high-tech materials played a large part in creating this racy configuration. Lightweight carbon fiber is starting to become popular, and it is used here for the air cleaner, Vance and Hines exhaust, and fenders. Kevlar is also finding a number of unconventional uses. For instance, all the brake lines and Barnett clutch plates on this road burner are made of Kevlar, courtesy of Goodrich in England.

Of course, a rear chain was adapted to the belt-driven motorcycle to allow for a large, sure-footed Avon tire to be mounted. The bike is light, agile, and handles as well as Tom expected when he set out to fashion a Harley into a twisty-road warrior.

I've often postulated the possibility of shaping a Harley into a hot-performing racing machine, but I have trouble with the tempting notion. Every time I begin to work a motorcycle into a racing configuration, a mind-melting apparition appears in my garage—a ghost so terrifying and unrelenting in its nature that I freeze in my tracks. A searing torrent pours from its fetid breath and the rafters of my garage are singed by the heat.

I know death is so near that I can taste it in my parched mouth as I attempt to speak. It halts me with a raised finger, crosses its muscled arms, and begins shaking its head. The massive mane of white hair and the long-flowing beard sway like the tide, while I attempt to beg for mercy. I shut up, my knees shaking like a handful of dice.

AVON AND TODD

Dual oil coolers on the white downtubes, the air dam and white powdercoating on the engine enhance a light appearance.

YEAR AND MAKE
1990 Harley-Davidson

OWNER
Tom Todd

MODEL
FXR

BUILDER
Tom Todd and G.T. Custom Cycles, Maryland, New York

ENGINE MODIFICATIONS
Crane ignition, RevTech pistons, RevTech heads, RevTech 40 cam, RevTech carburetor, Vance and Hines exhaust

TRANSMISSION MODIFICATIONS
Chain drive, powdercoated, hydraulic clutch

FINISH
Molding and paint by Kram of Cross Country Colors, white and blue lacquer, powdercoating by Sumax, urethane clear coat

FRAME MODIFICATIONS
Sumax and G.T. Custom Pro Comp chassis, single rear shock, alloy custom swingarm

FRONT END MODIFICATIONS
Showa forks, G.T. Custom Cycles fiberglass work

FEATURED
Easyriders, November 1995

Then a booming voice fills the garage and my tools fall to the deck from their pegboard hooks.

"You are an outlaw, and you will always ride choppers," it says. I can hear shingles sliding off the quaking roof. I attempt to argue and am immediately squelched. "Did I make myself clear?"

What can I say?

CHARITY RIDES IN... ON A BLACK BOYCE

The classic Kenny Boyce chassis with its FXR handling abilities, low-slung seating position, and tough-as-nails Harley tradition.

Here's another biker who has made something meaningful from a life that began as a drug-crazed, motorized maniac. That's right, folks, even criminals can make good. Yes, even men who make it their daily goals in life to sit on as many barstools as possible and to touch as many blondes as Antonio Banderas, can succeed.

Of course, Kenny Boyce has never done any of the above, and still he has built a motorcycle style that's respected the world over—the Kenny Boyce Pro Street.

In this case, the frame is the key. Don't ask me why or how, but his frames, for rubbermounted FXRs only, are a preferred frame replacement of more builders than any other chassis in the industry.

The frame is versatile and stylish without being spindly, and it fits. Take a look. The seating position is low. The scoot has a strong, healthy line and lends itself to performance, custom styling, or touring.

After making his mark in the industry for 20 years, Kenny gave something back with this particular example of the Boyce Pro Street look. This machine was specifically built for the *Easyriders* Juvenile Diabetes Foundation Sweepstakes.

But Kenny builds much more than just the frames. He finds the time to build complete machines such as this one, including high-performance engines and many unique Boyce components, when he's not sitting on barstools or caressing ... all right, I'll leave it alone.

The oil pressure gauge with miniature dash built in was an ingenious touch. The small lights indicate neutral and charging warnings.

Kenny's chassis include fenders, fuel tanks, polished aluminum oil tanks, and exhaust, for a light, winning combination. Just add front end and drive line for a white-knuckle ride.

YEAR AND MAKE
1994 Pro Street

OWNER
Kenny Boyce

MODEL
Pro Street

BUILDER
Kenny Boyce

ENGINE MODIFICATIONS
1994 80-cubic-inch FXR rebuilt by owner, heads ported by B.C. Gerolomy, Sifton 143 (550 lift) cam, Pro Street exhaust, Screamin' Eagle air cleaner

TRANSMISSION MODIFICATIONS
Andrews gears, Pro Street

FINISH
No molding, paint by Pro Street, black polyurethane, special paint by Carl Brouhard

FRAME MODIFICATIONS
Built by Boyce Pro Street Chassis Works, 32-degree rake, Pro Street offset swingarm, .095 tubing

FRONT END MODIFICATIONS
Marzocchi forks, Pro Street mid glide, billet aluminum triple trees

FEATURED
Easyriders, April 1995

EMERGENCY SPORTSTER

Here's a stock configured Sportster designed and built to handle winding roads and be aggressive on any straight-away. From the lightened Performance Machine wheels and brakes, to the XRV- modified engine, it's meant to go and look good doing it.

There's a rider on the staff who's 6-foot-4, lifts weights, rides big motorcycles, and does everything in a big, gruff way. But whenever he's pegged as unapproachable, he does something out of context, like get a set of tires for another crew member, loan another staff drunk the money to buy a bike, or help to find parts for a friend's project. So when a couple of women, one being a redhead, smoothed their way into the office flashing their "We're with the Red Cross" credentials and pearly white smiles, we dropped kernels of popcorn in the direction of Bandit's office.

He had recently purchased this Sportster, and since it fit him like a ouse-sized Killer Whale fits a ousehold fishbowl, we suspected hat Bandit had bought it to do omeone a favor. As it turned out, e accomplished two gracious goals. half-hour later the two girls left he office, and their smiles were ven broader than before.

Bandit had donated his high-performance Sportster to the Red Cross to help them raise funds. But Bandit doesn't deserve all the credit. It's his friends who helped make the once-883 Sportster come to life, including: Nempco, Roger Kallins at XRV Performance in Burbank, California, Storz, Headwinds, Performance Machine, and Mike Lisandro and Pamelina who painted it the appropriate colors. Just goes to show, he may be big—but he's soft. But don't tell him I said that. I'll be forced to leave the country.

There are no shortcuts taken in performance. It's a different school of thought at work here. Function is paramount with very little given up for style.

YEAR AND MAKE
1994 Harley-Davidson

OWNER
Bandit

MODEL
XRV

BUILDER
Roger Kallins

ENGINE MODIFICATIONS
Compu-Fire Elite 1, single-fire ignition, 1200cc, XRV-built engine, Axtell 9.5:1 heads, Axtell cam, QwikSilver carburetor, Nempco/Supertrapp exhaust, Pro-Fire Nology coils, HES coil mount, selectable electronic advance ignition module kit HDE-3, Hot Wires from Nology

TRANSMISSION MODIFICATIONS
Stores controls, XRV modifications

FINISH
Paint by Mike Lisandro, Red Cross colors in lacquer, special paint by Pamelina

FRAME MODIFICATIONS
Nempco progressive shocks

FRONT END MODIFICATIONS
39mm narrow glide with Nempco billet trees, XRV modified, Gold Valve cartridge emulators from Race Tech

FEATURED
Easyriders, October 1996

CHOPPERS RULE

THE VEHICLE FOR A RUGGED LIFESTYLE

The wild chopper encompasses everything *Easyriders* represents. It's the vehicle to a lifestyle. It's a fist-fighter on two wheels, the thief's iron steed, a womanizer in chrome. It's sex, drugs, and rock 'n' roll—with a throttle.

Initially, it was any motorcycle that an owner chopped, i.e. removed turn signals, fenders, lights, stock seats, fairings, or gaudy accessories. In the '50s riders began to bob Harleys by modifying the fenders, actually chopping them off. Originally, the term was "bobbed," which in the '60s became "chopped."

Modifications became more extreme in the '60s, and the aftermarket business blossomed around the lifestyle in the early '70s. Mad chopper artists were easily supplied with parts that assisted them in the unrelenting desire to take an original bulbous motorcycle and make it into something that spoke to the wild side of the streets.

Builders began using performance throttles to replace the sloppy and often-sluggish internal Harley throttles. In America, Flanders built handlebars for racing, and riders began to install them on their stock motorcycles. The early builders utilized hand tools and ingenuity to turn their machines from mild to wild. They cut the fenders by hand, removed parts, installed new handlebars, and modified their exhaust systems. They had bobbed their bikes.

In the '60s the trimming process flourished with cutting torches and bondo. Motorcycles were stripped to bare frames, unnecessary taps and brackets were trimmed away, then smoothed with bondo and repainted, usually to match the sheet metal paint scheme. Stock tanks were removed and replaced with smaller, more stylish units that showed off the grace and detail of the engines. Power plants were stripped and more components chromed. Wiring was hidden, bulky fenders were replaced with narrow ones, front ends were chromed, and highbars were installed. Not only was the motorcycle a hundred pounds lighter but it took on a whole new, menacing image: high voltage with a bare foot on wet pavement.

Then the '70s burst onto the scene and the world of choppers became a full-time business.

Easyriders magazine spread the word and broke the barriers. Companies began building long front ends, chromed sissybars, straight pipes, and modified frames. Within a couple of years the bikes that men carved out of bits and pieces, then rode like the wind, became the objects of catalogs. All of a sudden, a man could buy a bike and a truckload of accessories and retire to the garage for a month, and when he returned from that adjustable-wrench cave, he had a new machine. But that didn't transform a Harley into a righteous chopper. An attitude did.

Accessories built street customs, but torches and a hell-bent-for-leather attitude built choppers. Tight upper lips, impunity, too much whiskey, and fist fights built these long, lean, and mean machines. Breaking laws made choppers fast, loose women made 'em shiny, and freedom made them last.

THE FLEXIBLE RIGID

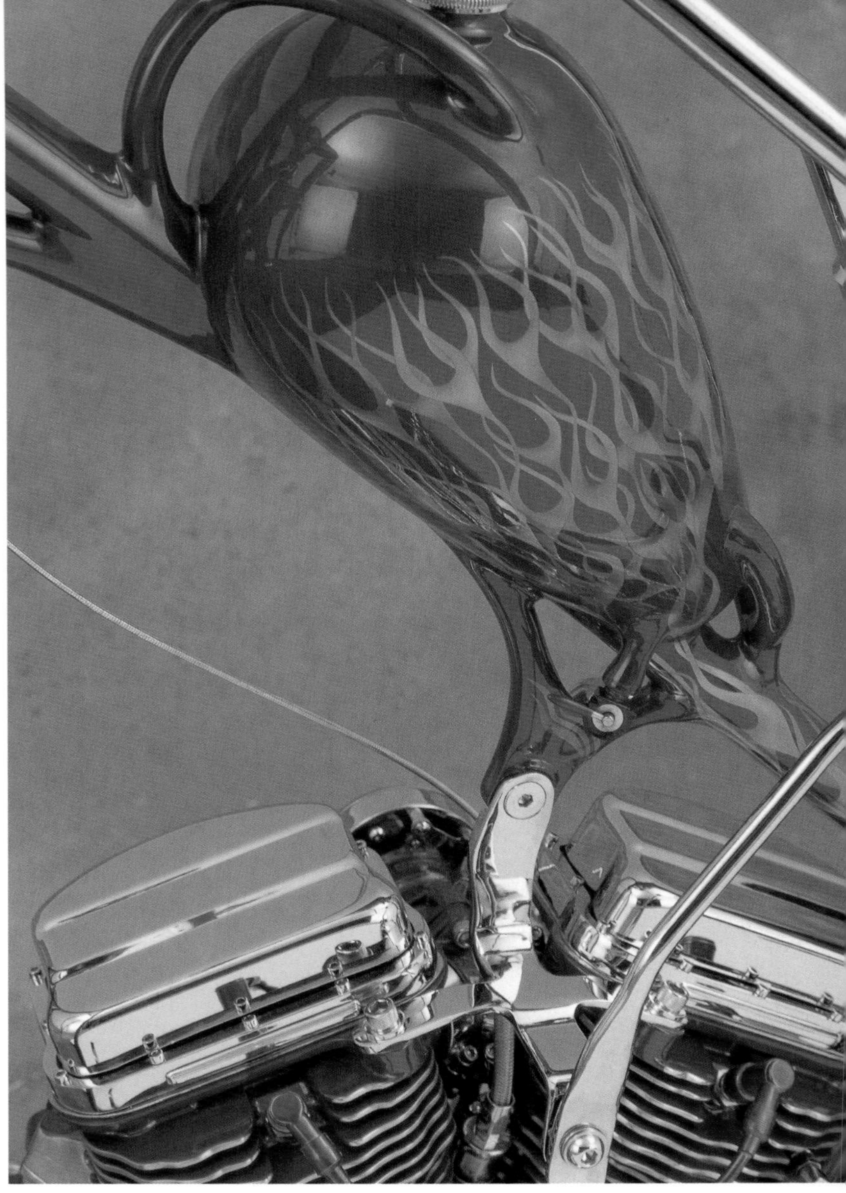

To say that this bike is worthy of the term "chopper" or even "radical chopper" is a gross understatement. It's so gross I should be penalized and forced to buy beer for the bros for a month. In fact, if you look up the word "radical" in the dictionary, there's probably a picture of this scoot and French bike builder Richard Piasecki. The 6-foot-8 owner of this stretched ride embodies every aspect of the '70s chopper rider through the creation of this carefully balanced, long-legged machine.

Years ago, the chopper builder/rider was one in the same. If you had a chop, you built it in your own back yard. If you were good, you built everything on the bike, and it had class. If the chop had class it was radical, individual, and tough to ride. This gangly machine is all of the above and more.

Richard built this and another equally radical ride in his basement over a four-year period. He spent thousands of hours bending tubes, welding, molding, and painting. His talents alone are responsible for 90 percent of this machine.

The bike began as a 1951 Panhead, and, other than the transmission, not much of the original motorcycle is left. Every bracket on the frame is handmade; all the seams are filled and molded with lead so no crack will ever appear.

He devised his own secondary transmission/jack shaft, featuring not one, but two chains and an intermediate sprocket allowing enough offset to run the wide rear rim in line with the front wheel. "Thanks to this setup the bike handles surprisingly well," says Richard. "The front forks are rigid, but, in fact, they flex slightly as I ride along—that's the only suspension I've got."

After completing both machines he loaded them in the back of his black Renault delivery van and shipped the to the United States where he met it a began a five-month odyssey across the country, and attending rallies to show the bikes. It wasn't the first time for Richard. A few years before, he broug radical bike to America and rode it fro coast to coast, scattering crowds with i look, causing traffic jams, emptying ba and scaring the hell out of regular citiz

Richard's wild ride meets every definition of radical. The look is radic

Even the fuel cell on this machine is a work of art. It's mounted carefully on the top rail of the frame, with sculpted braces matched by the form of the top motor mount.

Who knows how long the sissybar is, but aside from the rigid frame status, this bike would be one helluva ride for a passenger. Take a book and wrap a blanket around the rail.

with its 20-over stretched frame; the front end is suspension-less and extended 47 inches, and the rear section is stretched 8 inches. Radical is also synonymous with dangerous, and this bike has the rowdy look and feel caused by the addition of a highly dangerous open belt drive. Couple this with a suicide foot clutch and a jockey shift with a ratchet top, and suddenly the art of finding neutral in a panic situation becomes difficult, if not impossible.

Radical also has to do with the fact that this chopper was built to fit and serve one man. The bike is kick only and fired by a magneto, reinforcing the man's knowledge of his engine and skill with his right foot. Without a battery as back up, a magneto and one leg are delicate partners in finding the formula to get the beast started.

Richard is a man who knows every nut and bolt on his machine. He's a man who isn't afraid to stretch the limits of building a radical chopper, and he's willing to take his handmade creations from France to America and show them off to the toughest bunch of bikers in the world. I look forward to his next trip.

PIRELLI P6

Not only is this the most radical bike in the book, but Richard added elements such as a open belt drive with a painted belt, a suicide foot-clutch, and jockey hand-shift to add to the riding challenge.

This is actually a painted leather seat covered in clear vinyl. The taillights are hidden in the sculpted fender. Very clean.

Engine components are painted to match the color scheme of the frame. Close scrutiny of the engine reveal 93 inches of stroked power, ignited with a magneto and oiled with a late-model oil pump. There's very little of the original 1951 Harley-Davidson left here.

THE FLEXIBLE RIGID

The 54-degree rake of the frame was handled with the owner/builder's torches, an artistic eye, and lots of steel.

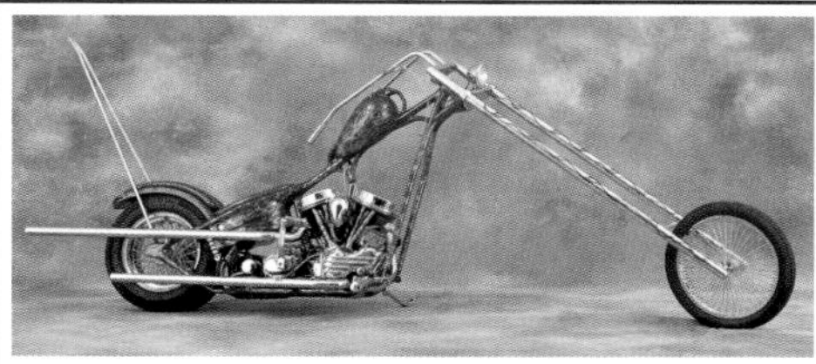

YEAR AND MAKE
1995 Pansecki

OWNER
Richard Piasecki

MODEL
Miss Liberty Panhead

ENGINE MODIFICATIONS
93-inch stroker, Morris Magneto, S&S lower end and pistons, Delkron cases, STD heads, Sifton cam, S&S "shorty" carburetor, owner-built exhaust, Sifton lifters

TRANSMISSION MODIFICATIONS
1951 box, 3-inch Primo belt, wheel sprocket acts as brake rotor

FINISH
Molding and paint by owner, dark red candy, flames, airbrushed mural and painted forks by owner

FRAME MODIFICATIONS
Chassis built by owner, 54-degree rake, 20-inch stretch

FRONT END MODIFICATIONS
47-inch over stock forks, painted tubes, suspension by flexion, engraved

FEATURED
Easyriders, May 1996

LUCKY STRIKE

Arlin Fatland is a legend in the industry, similar to Arlen Ness, yet the two are miles apart in many ways. Fatland got drunk every night, built bikes, and chased women until the next morning. Ness got drunk, built bikes, and stayed with the same woman for all those years. The outcome? Well, we won't go into that, except to say that Arlen Ness is very successful, has an entire line of world renowned products, and now his entire family works at the Ness facility.

Arlin Fatland has also been extremely successful. Though without a wife, he has always had a dedicated business partner, Jim Taylor. They recently celebrated their 25th anniversary in business together.

I better slow down. I could really mess this thing up and lose two close friends if I don't watch it. I suppose what I'm getting at is that in the '60s, some of us ruined our lives behind drugs, bikes, broads, and the mixture of it all. We lost our jobs, went to prison, left our wives. Hell, we had a blast. But reality sets in sooner or later, and, with or without knowing it, we made choices — or fell into a ditch. Or, if we were truly blessed by the chromed gods, we were open and sober when an opportunity came along that set us in a direction that saved our asses from the wino bin.

For Arlen Ness, I'm sure it was his partnership with his wife, Bev, that was his salvation. In a quiet, unassuming way, she's prevented Arlen from certain destruction any number of times and steered him on a course allowing him creative freedom, coupled with some semblance of business guidance.

Arlin Fatland also stumbled onto fortuity, whether Jim Taylor caused the opportunity to take place or not. Arlin and Jim started a shop in Denver called Two-Wheelers. As the years passed, they built a shop in Daytona, Florida, and later on in Sturgis, South Dakota. Arlin developed a line of products and sold them predominately through the pages of *Easyriders*.

So for both Arlen and Arlin, the motorcycle bug became a vocation, a thriving career coupled with a nonstop, hard-riding lifestyle. Both have survived and grown through the best and the worst of America's custom motorcycle history, and they're alive to tell about it. That's sayin' a lot.

There's another difference between the two. Arlin Fatland builds bikes like the one pictured here. They're tough, old, and built with parts from the past. Arlen Ness is a man with an innovative market to ride herd over, and it's imperative that he stays current. Arlin sells Arlen's parts to his customers, while building anything he pleases—such as 100-inch, all-chrome Knuckleheads. This motorcycle speaks of an era of tough hardtails, short hops, and outrunning cops. Maybe he should have found a wife like Bev Ness.

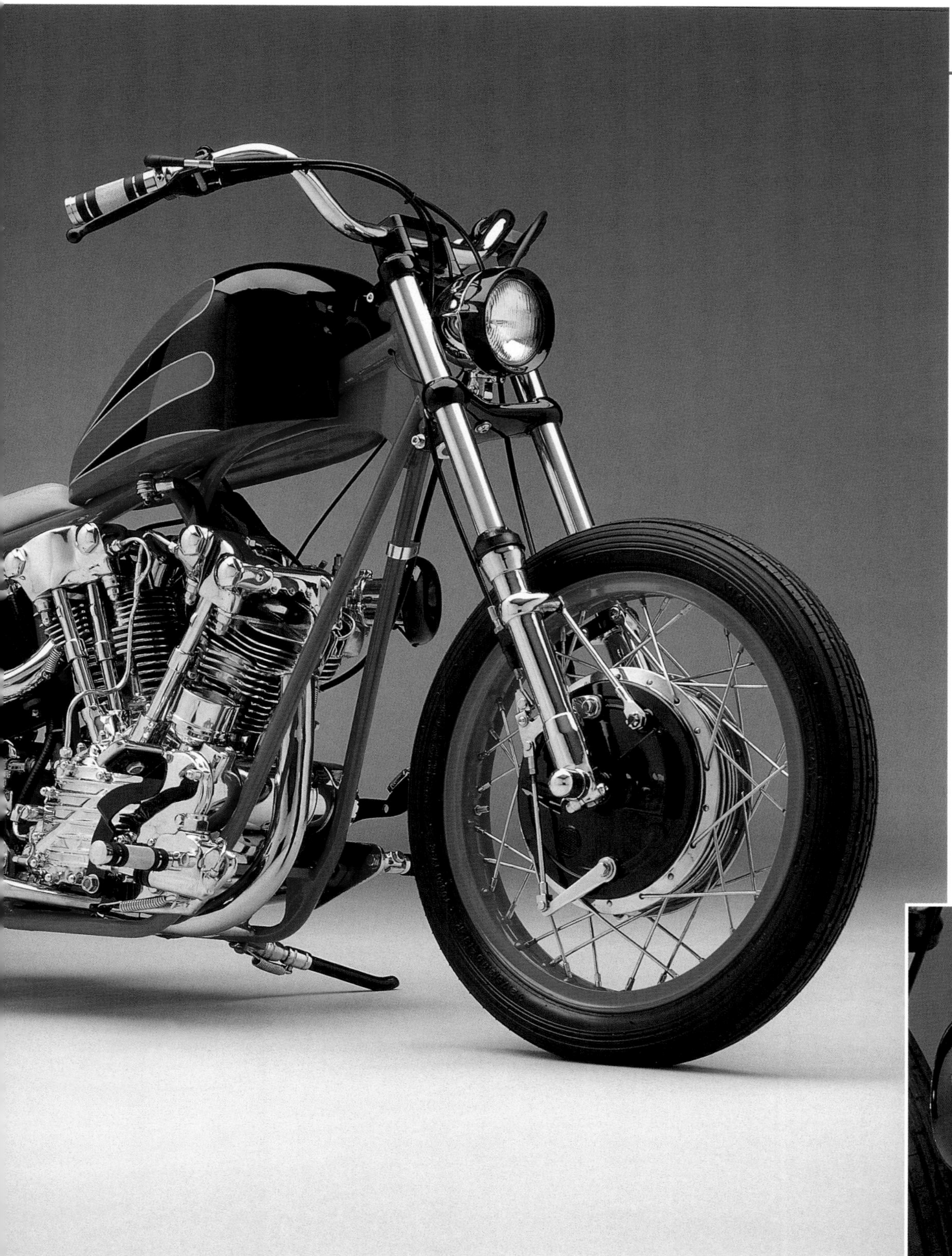

This machine is a mixing bowl of the old and new, the traditional chopper and a dirttrack racer with light wheels, racing forks, performance engine and bobbed rear fender.

Light and rowdy was once the order of the day, and this bike has it going on with the rigid frame, minuscule rear fender, solo seat, and tight handlebars.

The old and the new meet with GMA high-tech billet brakes, the historical 18-inch wire wheel, and the traditional painted-rim style.

A rare, completely chromed Knucklehead engine. Note the transmission cover and the machined fins on an otherwise smooth surface.

The extra frame strut on the rear section of the frame indicates that the chassis is prepared for serious horsepower.

YEAR AND MAKE
1942 Knucklehead

OWNER
Arlin Fatland

MODEL
EL

BUILDER
Steve Ruby

ENGINE MODIFICATIONS
American Cycle single-fire ignition, 100-cubic-inch stroker, S&S lower end, S&S pistons, cases chromed, heads chromed, S&S cam, S&S carburetor on the left side, Paughco exhaust

TRANSMISSION MODIFICATIONS
Andrews 5-speed, mainshafts and close-ratio gears

FINISH
Molding and painting by Paint By George, red, powdercoated frame

FRAME MODIFICATIONS
Ness rigid chassis, raked and stretched

FRONT END MODIFICATIONS
Road race Ceriani forks, Grimeca drum brakes, powdercoated trees

FEATURED
Easyriders, November 1995

PSYCHO PAN

There's something about bikers, real bikers, that is a cut above. We work harder, are smarter, and stream through more jobs, 'cause we won't put up with bullshit or lies. The nine-to-five life of the normal guy has never fit our creed. We either work extra hours or party. It's a no-bullshit existence. There's always another job for the hardworking or talented. For some, hard work pays off with a ticket to ride the bike of their dreams. J.S. Lambe is the perfect example of this kind of biker.

He made a solid living as a welder, but not an ordinary, sparks-in-your-face, rod-burning dude who drags out a job as long as he can. J.S. grabbed each job with a passion, took on extra assignments, worked long hours, and saved every nickel. He had a mission, and the only way he was going to get there was to stay true to his craft and his steadfast reputation as a welder. While the rest of us were fired for frequenting too many parties, J.S. stayed on the job with dogged determination, studied his *Easyriders* magazines, and made constant trips to the bank.

Every dog has his day, and for J.S., that day included seven boxes of Panhead parts and his MIG-welded vision of the perfect ride. After saving all that overtime credit, he still had to build his first bike himself. He shaved the frame while glancing over his shoulder at an *Easyriders* tech book. He ran all his wiring through the frame and even inside those sharp turn Z-bars. He split three fenders to create one just the way he wanted it, and meticulously put the entire beast together. Imagine Mr. Lambe wrenching away in his garage on the final assembly of a bike painted to match the blues, reds, and yellows he so often saw behind number 10 lenses while he lit a torch, sparked a weld, or cut through a sheet of steel. His brain filled with molten steel inspiration during hundreds of lost nights in dark spaces, with only his humming welder and a pile of rods as company, while the rest of use were cutting up the night, splitting chicks, lanes, and, well ... taking notes on the wild side.

Imagine the first day he fired up this explosion on two wheels and smelled the aroma of baking black wrinkle, the musty scent of seating asbestos linings, and heard the sound of his first V-twin warming to the road ahead. Imagine those shotgun/drags rattling the windows of his pad, the sense of power that surged through him as he flicked the quick throttle, and, finally, as he mounted her for that first ride, the vibration of freedom coursing through his bones, and the feel of his

This bike is all classic chopper lines, from the straight custom rigid frame, to the flat rear fender, to the Sportster tank.

The Panhead engine is one of the most beautiful V-twin Harley-Davidson engine configurations, especially when properly detailed.

hands on those bars so high. Imagine the rush as the toe of his boot pushed down on the shifter and he felt the Panhead jump into gear and the new clutch plates grab.

He'd waited way too long for this day. As the 21-inch front wheel left the pavement for the initial blast and a young woman tried to get his attention from inside a diner, he realized he had a helluva lot of catching up to do.

The owner chose to stay consistent with the '70s style, including the standard shift mechanism and straight foot pegs, although the vibration-free Isotomer pegs were released in the '90s

The shotgun, straight-pipe exhaust was one of the best-looking systems to be designed for Harleys. It pulls the pipes away from the looks of the engine and enhances the line of the bike.

The rear wheel is standard for the '70s, an all-chrome, 16-inch spoked wheel with drum brakes.

YEAR AND MAKE
1957 Harley-Davidson

OWNER
J.S. Lambe

MODEL
FLH

BUILDER
Owner, Hutch, Gene

ENGINE MODIFICATIONS
Rebuilt by Danny Johnson (Johnson Performance), Sifton cam, S&S Super E carburetor, Custom Chrome exhaust, special thanks to Piedmont Cycle and Wayne's Automotive

TRANSMISSION MODIFICATIONS
Andrews gears, ratchet top, chrome

FINISH
Molding by owner, painted by Barry McBride, Dupont hot hues, psychedelic stripes

FRAME MODIFICATIONS
Paughco rigid chassis, 36-degree rake, 4-inch stretch

FRONT END MODIFICATIONS
6-inch-over tubes, turned and chromed lower legs

FEATURED
Easyriders, October 1995

ATTENTION TO DETAIL

I got drunk last night and danced with death as my motorcycle doused itself with gasoline while on a steep decline leading to a very busy cross street. If I had slid into the on-coming traffic on a suicide-stricken motorcycle, I would have surely burst into flames, and been run over by several speeding, blind-to-my-plight motorists, who would have later testified that they never saw the spinning ball of flames. The police officer would have agreed that the explosion the size of a hand grenade was difficult for the average citizen to view, and, besides, I'm only a motorcyclist. Never deserved to live anyway.

It's a wonder builders the level of Mike Maldonado and owner Craig Cagle spend two and a half years of their lives creating a bike the caliber of this one, if their lives and creative accomplishments are in such dire danger once free to roam the highways of the world. Yes, it's a wonder, but we wouldn't have it any other way. Mike is just beginning his career as a top builder, yet every bike he builds is a creative masterpiece and a tribute to his talents, whether it lasts for minutes or he rides it for years. The creative process never stops. Thank God.

Long black and bad is the virtual essence behind this Mike Muldanado creation for Craig Cagle. Minimalist design, lotsa chrome and a truck load of class.

ATTENTION TO DETAIL

100 cubic inches of Harley-Davidson power unleashed on the Andrews gear box via a massive open belt drive system. More menacing than a stuck wide open chain say the open belt screams with shear terror to a leather covered ankle inches away.

YEAR AND MAKE
1996 Harley-Davidson

OWNER
Craig Cagle

MODEL
Hardtail

BUILDER
Owner and Mike Maldonado

ENGINE MODIFICATIONS
93-inch S&S motor, Dyna S ignition, S&S pistons and lower end, Sputhe cases, STD heads, Sifton cam, S&S Super G carburetor, Rod Sexton exhaust

TRANSMISSION MODIFICATIONS
Andrews gears, Primo engine and trans sprocket, Tolle wheel sprocket

FINISH
Painted and molded by Mike Maldonado, black urethane

FRAME MODIFICATIONS
Modified Paughco chassis, 50-degree rake, 5-inch stretch.

FRONT END MODIFICATIONS
Kennedy adjustable wide glide trees, Tolle forks, 18 inches over stock

FEATURED
Easyriders, December 1996

Classic spoke wheels carry the chain driven chopper through the narrow lanes of Southern California freeways and terrorize it's citizenry

ALTER EGO

This chop is a goddamn fruit salad of variations from the anti-rule-book of building the devils of the night. That's a mouthful, and if you're not in the hangover state I'm in, you probably won't understand a single word. So, I will attempt to explain.

Generally this bike is neat, exciting, and interesting, from the massive stretched frame, to the wild exhaust shooting out both sides of the bike, to the crisp paint scheme. But look closer and you'll discover items usually not found on wild choppers, like the painted rims, the engine finish that's almost straight off several stock bikes, but mixed (no glistening fully polished or chrome motor here, yet it's sharp), and the gas tank that looks fine at a glance, but under

The engine detailing is absolutely clean, yet frugal in its execution. Note the black cases, the stock finish on the barrels, and the bead-blasted finish on the heads.

microscopic evaluation should have been stretched to better fit the frame.

Chuck Hamm of Dinosaurs Unlimited in Warren, Oregon, doesn't have the multitude of talents at his fingertips that many builders do, yet he built a jockey- shift chopper that makes people stop in their tracks, and he didn't spend a fortune following the customizer's guide book in the process. You know, the book of no rules.

The Sportster tank has been modified to hide the mounting hardware sanitizing the assembly and enhancing the lines of the frame.

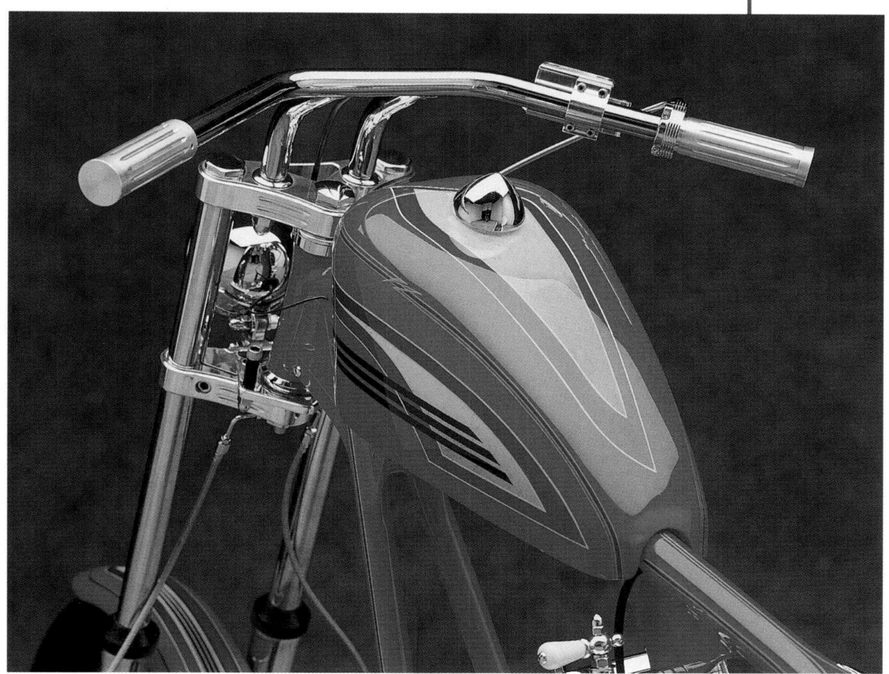

This is considered a long bike in custom circles, due to the stretch in the frame downtubes that visually lowers the seat height and raises the tank, demanding a long front end to reach the ground.

YEAR AND MAKE
1990 Harley-Davidson

OWNER
George Jones

MODEL
Dinosaur

BUILDER
Chuck Hamm of Dinosaurs Unlimited

ENGINE MODIFICATIONS
Crane single-fire ignition, RevTech pistons, RevTech heads, RevTech 40 cam, SU carburetor, 2-inch Dinosaur exhaust, Baisley balancing, Python II baffles

TRANSMISSION MODIFICATIONS
Jockey shift by Dinosaurs, Primo 3-inch belt drive

FINISH
Molding and paint by Gary Welter, smooth red paint, graphics by Dave, Don Aperson pinstriping

FRAME MODIFICATIONS
Dinosaurs modified Softail, 33-degree rake, stretched 6 inches up and 4 inches forward

FRONT END MODIFICATIONS
Dinosaurs modified wide glide, 9-inches over stock, shaved lower legs

FEATURED
Easyriders, October 1995

COSMIC CHOPPER

Ah, the tyrannical image of the chopper. "Ride the best or die with the rest," Louie Falcigno mutters in his 20-year-old chop shop on the coast of Florida. The tropical wind whistles off the Atlantic and through the rattling tin building, whipping Louie into a fanatical frenzy. As the shop threatens to leave its earthly foundation, Louie screams, his three-foot-long gray beard flying parallel to the cracking concrete deck, "Choppers forever, forever choppers."

Outside the wind calms down, as if it knows that no one will ever stop this man from his mission, which Louie declares is "to build choppers no one will ever forget." It takes him a solid year to build the chassis and the myriad of handmade parts that brand his bikes truly one-of-a-kind. He then lashes Billy Streeter to a case of Jack Daniel's, and for two months of seven-day work weeks Billy paints what Louie imagines.

You might wonder what's in this mad master's multi-colored (except for green) mind. Louie imagines a world of wild, wanton women; unrelenting rock 'n' roll; fist-fighting, knife-wielding violence; and anarchy on two wheels. In other words, fun. He hallucinates of wilder times, cops he could outrun, terrified small towns with no phones, and nights of unlimited debauchery. Same dream I have.

Nothing extra added on this machine. No indicator lights or turn signals. The primary belt is open and menacing, the pipes long and straight.

COSMIC CHOPPER

A classic chopper, all-mean and nasty, built for danger and speed with little concern for creature comforts, although I spotted an electric starter on this one.

YEAR AND MAKE
1994 Cosmic Chopper

OWNER
Lou Falcigno

MODEL
Chopper

BUILDER
C&L Hog Shop, Fort Pierce, Florida

ENGINE MODIFICATIONS
96-cubic-inch S&S motor, Dyna ignition, S&S pistons and lower end, S&S cases, Mega-Performance heads, EV4 cam, S&S carburetor, C&L exhaust

TRANSMISSION MODIFICATIONS
Sputhe 5-speed, jockey shift, two belt drives, SuperMax rear pulley

FINISH
Molding and painting by Jack Beasely, every color but green lacquer, Billy Streeter special paint

FRAME MODIFICATIONS
Atlas modified by C&L, 4-inch stretch, 3/4-inch rake

FRONT END MODIFICATIONS
2-inch over tubes, chrome, custom master cylinder

FEATURED
Easyriders, December 1995

SUGAR BEAR RETURNS

Sugar Bear is a contemporary builder who is brave enough to bring back the drug-induced times and designs of the '70s. Note the gooseneck frame, the extreme rake, the long custom springer front end, and the wild rockers on the axle.

As you might imagine from reading the molten mad talk contained in this fire-breathing book, the '60s and '70s were wild. Actually, they were beyond unrestrained, uncontrolled, mad, crazy, or ferocious. They were downright dangerous, hairy, and hazardous! Some of the brothers died, some went to prison, and some settled down. Still others said, "I'm outta here."

Sugar Bear did just that. He looked around one morning in the mid-'70s, and since no one was looking back, and the recession had hit, he made his move. Gas went from 25 cents a gallon to a buck and a half. Harley was building Super Glides, and the cops weren't at his door, so Sugar Bear closed his shop and slipped quietly into family life.

But deep inside his gut, his blood still boiled for the old days of, well ... it's just too terrifying to mention. When he resurfaced, he built this tribute to the old days on the streets of Hollywood and proceeded to blow minds. Today's riders look at him askance and wonder what alien planet he's from. The old-timers, on the other hand, study his machines and a chill streaks up their spines, a streak of fear, bad drug deals, and treachery. Then they smile with recognition and wait for Sugar Bear to build another one.

SUGAR BEAR RETURNS

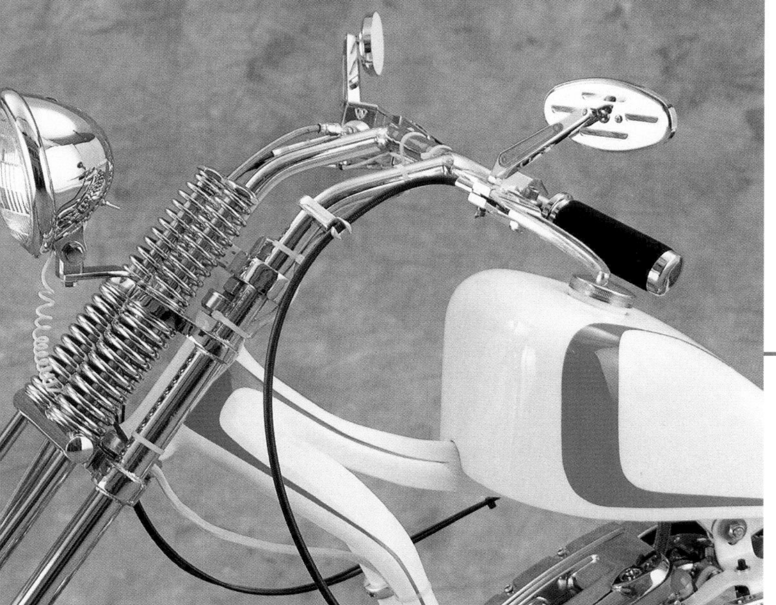

Gooseneck frames kicked off a line of handlebars that are popular today—handlebars with risers built in, bent back to bring the bars to the rider.

As you can see, this machine is low, lean, and long, a tradition born in the '70s. By today's standards this bike is a rugged ride, yet if the right guy builds one, choppers can handle well.

YEAR AND MAKE
1986 Harley-Davidson

OWNER
Sugar Bear

MODEL
Chopper

BUILDER
Sugar Bear

ENGINE MODIFICATIONS
Branch heads, powdercoated cylinders, egg-shaped cam, S&S E carburetor, Paughco exhaust, stroked and polished

TRANSMISSION MODIFICATIONS
Backcut gears, Super Max belt drive systems

FINISH
Molded and painted by Sugar Bear, white, orange lacquer and urethane, Quality powdercoating

FRAME MODIFICATIONS
Harley-Davidson and Luna Welding, stretched 4 inches here and 3 inches there, fender ears removed

FRONT END MODIFICATIONS
25-inch-over springer

FEATURED
Easyriders, March 1996

CODGER DODGER

Note the front end and how clean it looks. Everything is designed to match, even when the builder buys from several sources such as Ness triple trees, Tolle tubes, and Performance Machine, wheels, brakes, controls, and rotors.

Eddie Trotta, the man behind this late-model, chopped, bad ass bike, lives in a blistering, urban nightmare. It's a city fulla drivers who can't hear, can't see, and randomly turn in front of motorcyclists. Turn signals? These drivers have never heard of 'em. Where is this hellhole of incompetent road slugs? It's a retirement haven on the Florida coast.

Eddie's instinct for survival quickly developed four codes for enduring the onslaught of mindless retirees. First, a chop must be loud, and he handled that with MAC pipes. Next, a brother needs speed, so his bikes are bare bones, light, and sport seriously pumped and stroked motors. Don't forget bright. Eddie makes the chrome shine and the paint glitter.

And finally, Eddie builds wild motorcycles that handle well in order to dodge errant drivers who are asleep at the wheel.

Most of us city dwellers understand the hazards of rush hour traffic, Sunday margarita drinkers, and truck drivers concentrating solely on delivery deadlines. We also know the pitfalls of the open road: wandering cattle, low flying birds, hordes of insects, lost truckers, and locals who never learned the meaning of stop signs.

It's a nasty world out there for the freedom seeking chopper rider who would rather risk his life in the saddle than wait for a heart attack while sitting on the couch. If you're gonna live, do it with style.

Eddie is talented at pulling all the elements together, like the stretched frame and matching stretched tanks, the trimmed rear fender, and all the necessary custom components.

CODGER DODGER

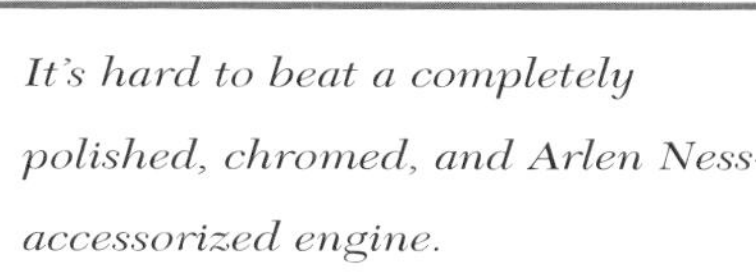

It's hard to beat a completely polished, chromed, and Arlen Ness-accessorized engine.

YEAR AND MAKE
1995 Thunder Cycle

OWNER
Eddie Trotta

MODEL
Chopped Softail

BUILDER
Thunder Cycle Designs, Fort Lauderdale, Florida

ENGINE MODIFICATIONS
98-inch S&S motor, Dyna ignition, S&S pistons and lower end, polished cases, STD heads, EV 57 cam, S&S G carburetor, Mac pipes, JIMS lifters

TRANSMISSION MODIFICATIONS
Andrews gears

FINISH
Molding by Jim, painting by Joe Earl, violet paint from House of Kolor, aluminum leaf special paint

FRAME MODIFICATIONS
Atlas Pro Magnum chassis, wide drive for rear wheel, 38-degree rake, 4-inch stretch, internal fender struts

FRONT END MODIFICATIONS
Ness trees, 4-inch-over tubes

FEATURED
Easyriders, March 1996

WHY SIMPLE AIN'T EASY

This bare bones bike is the epitome of cleanliness. The rigid frame is clean, the paint job simple. There's no electric starter, bulky battery, or even a passenger seat and pegs. He's going alone.

Time and money equals motion, but it usually doesn't happen that easy. Most guys building their first bike, like Andy here, figure they'll save for a couple of years, buy some parts—done deal. Andy scrimped on women and scotch, saved beer cans and newspapers, and made wise investments. Finally one day, Andy strolled into George Karapetian's All Star Cycles with his jug of change and said, "Here's the money. I wanna ride."

George immediately recognized the virus Andy was stricken with and quickly checked him in for therapy, introduced him to chopper rehab, and entered him into a series of lessons on the biker's Code of The West. Andy responded to the therapy quickly and soon was asking George responsible questions and respecting his decisions regarding the construction of this motorcycle. He began to understand that first there is a frame, then there is a chassis prepped and ready for paint. He learned that no off-the-shelf fuel cell would do and needed modification before it was truly custom and fit the style of the frame.

A quick study, Andy was back on the streets in no time, watching George turn his hard-earned cash into something that makes men's hearts swell with pride. He's now the owner of a classic, kick-only chop. He wouldn't have it any other way

Open primary belt drives add something to any custom. They enhance the performance appearance and make adjustment a breeze. Note that the chain sprocket doubles as the disc brake rotor.

YEAR AND MAKE
1994 Harley-Davidson

OWNER
Andy Magdesian

MODEL
Special Construction Chop

BUILDER
Greg, All Star Cycles

ENGINE MODIFICATIONS
96-inch S&S motor, Crane single-fire ignition, Crane 561 cam, S&S Super E carburetor, Porker pipes

TRANSMISSION MODIFICATIONS
Rebuilt by Sand's Racing, kicker only, Andrews gears

FINISH
Molded by All Star, painted by Peter Johansson, purple pearl by House Of Kolor, candy purple ghost flames

FRAME MODIFICATIONS
Frame by Atlas and All Star, rigid, 1/5-inch rake, 1-inch stretch, welds filled and smoothed, mounts hidden

FRONT END MODIFICATIONS
Billet wide glide, 4 inches over

FEATURED
Easyriders, April 1996

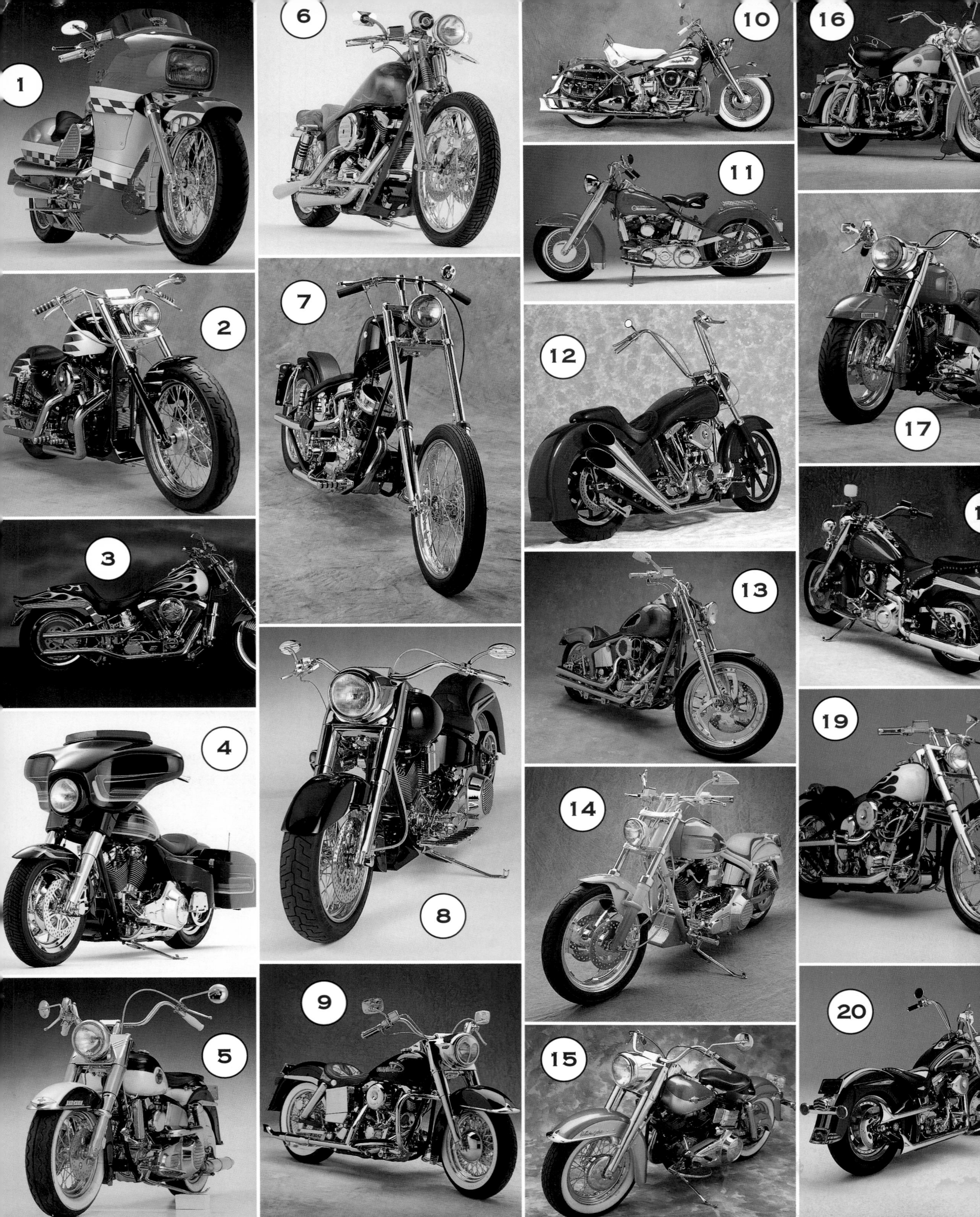
1
2
3
4
5
6
7
8
9
10
11
12
13
14
15
16
17
19
20

GALLERY

1 1989 FXR. Owner Arnie Araujo, featured in *Easyriders* July 1996.

2 1988 XL. Owner Bruce LeFevre featured in *Easyriders* July 1995.

3 1990 Softail Custom. Owner Al Pino, featured in *Easyriders* August 1995.

4 FLHTC Ultra. Owner Grady Pfeiffer, featured in *Easyriders* April 1995.

5 1958 FL Electra-Glide. Owner Dan Dearborn, featured in *Easyriders* October 1996.

6 1993 Dyna Glide. Owner Tony Carlini, featured in *Easyriders* March 1995.

7 FL Panhead. Owner Mike Trussell, featured in *Easyriders* August 1995.

8 1988 FLST Softail. Owner Jerry Potter, featured in *Easyriders* July 1996.

9 1975 FLH Shovelhead. Owner Phillene Tarone, featured in *Easyriders* August 1995.

10 1956 FLHF Panhead. Owner Jim Hansen, featured in Easyriders July 1996.

11 1950 FL Panhead. Owner Don Butler, featured in *Easyriders* January 1995.

12 1967 Chopper Shovelhead. Owner Dean Medico, featured in *Easyriders* March 1995.

13 1992 FXST. Owner K Mishler, featured in *Easyriders* June 1995.

14 1994 Evolution. Featured in *Easyriders* December 1996.

15 1965 Electra-Glide. Owner Frank Davis, feaured in *Easyriders* April 1996.

16 1958 FLH Panhead. Owner Mike Cleary, featured in *Easyriders* August 1996.

17 1989 FXST. Owner Daniel Stern, featured in *Easyriders* July 1995.

18 1982 FLH Shovelhead. Owner Jeff Sundberg, featured in *Easyriders* September 1995.

19 1979 Shovelhead. Owner Mike Rimpley, featured in *Easyriders* March 1995.

20 1990 Fat Boy. Owner Eddie Kirmiss, featured in *Easyriders* February 1996.

21 1995 Softail. Owner Walter Rios, featured in *Easyriders* October 1995.

22 1992 Heritage Softail. Owner Paul Pardini, featured in *Easyriders* October 1995.

23 1942 UL Flathead. Owner Eric Neubecker, featured in *Easyriders* February 1996.

24 1991 FXR Low Rider. Featured in *Easyriders* November 1996.

25 1971 Rigid Shovel. Owner Paul Whitaker, featured in *Easyriders* September 1996.

PICTURE CREDITS

Exclusive photographs from the archives of *Easyriders*:

The publishers would like to acknowledge the following photographers:

3	Raiko Hartman
4 cr	Michael Lichter
4 tl	Michael Lichter
5 b	Michael Lichter
5 r	Raiko Hartman
5 t	Michael Lichter
6 b	Jean Marie Boissier
6 t	Michael Lichter
7 bl	Michael Lichter
7 br	Michael Lichter
7 t	Raiko Hartman
8 bl	Dennis Evans
8 cl	Michael Lichter
8 tl	Michael Lichter
9 br	Michael Lichter
9 cr	Michael Lichter
9 tc	Raiko Hartman
9 tr	Michael Lichter
9bc	Raiko Hartman
10-15	Michael Lichter
16-19	Michael Lichter
20-23	Michael Lichter
24-25	Raiko Hartman
26-27	Chuck Emery
28-29	Scott Cunningham
30-31	Michael Lichter
32-33	Michael Lichter
34-35	Raiko Hartmann
36-37	Raiko Hartman
38-39	Dennis Evans
40-41	Raiko Hartman
42-43	Dennis Evans
44-45	Raiko Hartman
46-47	Michael Lichter
48-49	Raiko Hartman
50-51	Michael Lichter
52-53	Michael Lichter
54-55	Michael Lichter
56-57	Michael Lichter
58-59	John Wycoff
60-61	Raiko Hartman
62-63	Dennis Evans
64-65	Raiko Hartman
66-67	Raiko Hartman
68-69	Michael Lichter
70-71	Michael Lichter
72-73	Raiko Hartman
74 bl	Michael Lichter
74 c	Michael Lichter
74 t	Michael Lichter
75 b	Don Rogers
75 c	Michael Lichter
75 t	Bob Jones
76-81	Michael Lichter
82-85	Michael Lichter
86-89	Bob Jones
90-91	Michael Lichter
92-93	Don Rogers
94-95	Michael Lichter
96 b	Michael Lichter
96 c	Michael Lichter
96 t	Carl Wilson
97 b	Michael Lichter
97 cl	Raiko Hartman
97 cr	Michael Lichter
97 t	Michael Lichter
98-103	Michael Lichter
104-107	Don Rogers
108-111	John Wycoff
112-113	Michael Lichter
114-115	Don Rogers
116-117	Raiko Hartman
118-119	Carl Wilson
120-121	Michael Lichter
122-123	Michael Lichter
124-125	Michael Lichter
126 b	Michael Lichter
126 c	Markus Cuff
126 t	Jean Marie Boissier
127 b	Michael Lichter
127 c	Dennis Evans
127 tr	Markus Cuff
127tc	Michael Lichter
128-133	Michael Lichter
134-137	Jean Marie Boissier
138-141	Michael Lichter
142-143	Dennis Evans
144-145	Markus Cuff
146 b	Michael Lichter
146 c	Don Rogers
146 t	Raiko Hartman
147 b	Raiko Hartman
147 c	John Wycoff
147 t	Michael Lichter
148-153	Raiko Hartman
154-157	Michael Lichter
158-161	Michael Lichter
162-163	John Wycoff
164-165	Michael Lichter
166-167	Don Rogers
168-169	Raiko Hartman
170-171	Don Rogers
172-173	Michael Lichter
174-175	Scott Cunningham (25)

Bill Ellis (11)
Chuck Emery (23)
Raiko Hartman (1, 4, 5, 6, 7, 8, 17)
Michael Lichter (9, 10, 16, 18, 19, 22, 24)
Stephen Ogilvy (12)
Don Rogers (13, 14, 15, 20, 21)
Silvermoon (2)
John Wycoff (3)

Every effort has been made to acknowledge each phtographer and picture correctly, and Carlton Books Limited apologises for any unintentional errors or omissions, which will be corrected in future editions of this book.